^{THE} Knitted Home

THE
Knitted Home

Hand-knitted projects room by room

SIAN BROWN

GUILD OF MASTER CRAFTSMAN PUBLICATIONS

First published 2011 by
Guild of Master Craftsman Publications Ltd
Castle Place, 166 High Street, Lewes,
East Sussex BN7 1XU

ISBN 978-1-86108-807-9

Publisher: Jonathan Bailey
Production Manager: Jim Bulley
Managing Editor: Gerrie Purcell
Senior Project Editor: Virginia Brehaut
Copy Editor: Lorraine Slipper
Managing Art Editor: Gilda Pacitti
Art Editor: Rebecca Mothersole
Photographer: Tim Clinch

Set in Kozuka Gothic
Colour origination by GMC Reprographics
Printed and bound in China by Hing Yip Printing Co. Ltd

Contents

Introduction

The home is one of the most important things in our lives after the people close to us. It is a sanctuary where we relax and escape from the world, where we spend time with family and friends. It is the place that reflects our personalities and our tastes, and provides us with a comforting and comfortable environment to live in. Everyone's idea of home will be different, but it means the same to all of us.

The idea behind this book was to put together projects for different rooms of the home. The designs reflect the elements that make a home welcoming: the familiar look of handmade things with a nostalgic feeling of childhood memories. Each item also reflects the things I love about design; focusing on a use of colour and texture, starting with traditional ideas and adding individual and sometimes quirky elements. Most of the yarns are pure fibres, and the patterns use a variety of techniques and skill levels.

Each room has its own theme and the inspiration has come from a variety of different places, starting with what I see around my own home on the coast.

Walking along the beach in both summer and winter gave me the ideas for the seaside themes in the lounge, the bathroom and the pirate's bedroom. Looking at gardens filled with summer flowers, going to markets and growing plants all provided the theme for the kitchen and garden, with richly coloured autumn berries and flowers for the dining room. The main and guest bedrooms have a traditional and retro feel, they are tactile and welcoming. The nursery and secret garden bedroom were created from memories of my daughters' childhoods.

I hope that this book will help to inspire you to create unique and individual projects, finding elements within the ten room themes and seasons that will work well in your own home.

Sian Brown

Lounge

THE STUNNING, WINDSWEPT **COAST IN WINTER** PROVIDES THE INSPIRATION FOR THIS ROOM. USING A SOFT, **NATURAL PALETTE** AND **CHUNKY** YARNS, THESE **TACTILE**, COZY PROJECTS WILL HELP KEEP THE WINTER CHILLS AWAY.

Winter

Knotted rope cable throw

Felted storage containers

Pebbles draught excluder

coast

Knotted rope
cable throw

Soft, chunky pure wool is used in a warm but neutral colour for this gorgeous throw. The large knotted cable, zigzag with bobbles and four-stitch cable give it a deeply textured feel for warmth and comfort in the lounge.

YOU WILL NEED

Garnstudio Eskimo, 100% wool
(54yd/49m per 50g ball)
26 balls Light Beige Mix (shade 047)
1 pair 9mm (US13:UK00) needles
1 circular 9mm (US13:UK00) needle
1 cable needle

FINISHED SIZE

Approx. 41in (104cm) wide x 41in (104cm) long

TENSION

10 sts and 14 rows to 4in (10cm) over st st using 9mm needles.

CABLE PANEL A
(worked over 32 sts)

Row 1: (WS) P2, k6, p6, k4, p6, k6, p2.
Row 2: K2, p6, C6F, p4, C6F, p6, k2.
Row 3: As row 1.
Row 4: K2, p4, (Cr4R, p2, Cr4L) twice, p4, k2.
Row 5: P2, k4, p3, k4, p6, k4, p3, k4, p2.
Row 6: K2, p3, Cr4R, p4, C6B, p4, Cr4L, p3, k2.
Row 7: P2, k3, p3, k5, p6, k5, p3, k3, p2.
Row 8: K2, p2, Cr4R, p5, k6, p5, Cr4L, p2, k2.
Row 9: P2, k2, p3, k6, p6, k6, p3, k2, p2.
Row 10: K2, p2, Cr4L, p5, k6, p5, Cr4R, p2, k2.
Row 11: As row 7.
Row 12: K2, p3, Cr4L, p4, C6B, p4, Cr4R, p3, k2.
Row 13: As row 5.
Row 14: K2, p4, (Cr4L, p2, Cr4R) twice, p4, k2.
Row 15: As row 1.
Row 16: As row 2.
Row 17: As row 1.
Row 18: K2, p6, k3, Cr4L, k2, Cr4R, k3, p6, k2.
Row 19: P2, k6, p3, k2, p6, k2, p3, k6, p2.
Row 20: K2, p6, C5L, C6B, C5R, p6, k2.
Row 21: P2, k8, p12, k8, p2.
Row 22: K2, p8, (C6F) twice, p8, k2.
Row 23: As row 21.
Row 24: K2, p6, Cr5R, C6B, Cr5L, p6, k2.
Row 25: As row 19.
Row 26: K2, p6, k3, Cr5R, Cr5L, k3, p6, k2.
Rows 1 to 26 form cable panel A and are repeated.

CABLE PANEL B
(worked over 36 sts)

Row 1: (WS) P2, k3, p6, k9, p2, k3, p6, k3, p2.
Row 2: K2, p3, k6, p3, Cr3L, p8, k6, p3, k2.
Row 3 and every foll WS row: Knit or purl sts as now set.
Row 4: K2, p3, C6F, p4, Cr3L, p7, C6B, p3, k2.
Row 6: K2, p3, k6, p5, Cr3L, p6, k6, p3, k2.
Row 8: K2, p3, k6, p6, Cr3L, p5, k6, p3, k2.
Row 10: K2, p3, C6F, p7, Cr3L, p4, C6B, p3, k2.
Row 12: K2, p3, k6, p5, MB, p2, Cr3L, p3, k6, p3, k2.
Row 14: K2, p3, k6, p8, Cr3R, p3, k6, p3, k2.
Row 16: K2, p3, C6F, p7, Cr3R, p4, C6B, p3, k2.
Row 18: K2, p3, k6, p6, Cr3R, p5, k6, p3, k2.
Row 20: K2, p3, k6, p5, Cr3R, p6, k6, p3, k2.
Row 22: K2, p3, C6F, p4, Cr3R, p7, C6B, p3, k2.
Row 24: K2, p3, k6, p3, Cr3R, p2, MB, p5, k6, p3, k2.
Rows 1 to 24 form cable panel B and are repeated.

THROW
Centre panel A (make 1)
Using 9mm needles cast on 32 sts.
Work from panel A until work measures 38$\frac{1}{2}$in (98cm), ending with a wrong-side row.
Cast off.

Left side panel A (make 1)
Using 9mm needles cast on 33 sts.
Row 1: (WS) P3, k6, p6, k4, p6, k6, p2.
Row 2: K2, p6, C6F, p4, C6F, p6, k3.
These 2 rows set the patt with 3 sts in st st at left-hand side.
Work from panel A until work measures 38$\frac{1}{2}$in (98cm), ending with a wrong-side row.
Cast off.

Right side panel A (make 1)

Using 9mm needles cast on 33 sts.
Row 1: (WS) P2, k6, p6, k4, p6, k6, p3.
Row 2: K3, p6, C6F, p4, C6F, p6, k2.
These 2 rows set the patt with 3 sts in st st at right-hand side.
Work from panel A until work measures 38¹/₂in (98cm), ending with a wrong-side row.
Cast off.

Centre panel B
(make 2)

Using 9mm needles cast on 36 sts.
Work from panel B until work measures 38¹/₂in (98cm), ending with a wrong-side row.
Cast off.

FINISHING

Join panels together.

Top edging

With right side facing using circular needle, pick up and k116 sts across cast-off edges.
Next row: Knit to end.
Next row: K1, m1, k to last st, m1, k1.
Rep the last 2 rows once more.
Cast off knitwise.

Bottom edging

With right side facing using circular needle, pick up and k116 sts across cast-on edges.
Next row: K to end.
Next row: K1, m1, k to last st, m1, k1.
Rep the last 2 rows once more.
Cast off knitwise.

Side edgings
(alike)

With right side facing using circular needle, pick up and knit 116 sts along side edges.
Next row: K to end.
Next row: K1, m1, k to last st, m1, k1.
Rep the last 2 rows once more.
Cast off knitwise.
Join corners.

Alternatives

This throw is made in panels, so any number and length can be made to vary the size. A cushion cover can also be made by combining panels to form a square and adding a stocking-stitch back.

Felted
storage containers

A soft, chunky wool in cool wintery colours and a simple double cable is used for these containers. Felting makes the knitting firm and adds to the soft and cozy look.

YOU WILL NEED

Debbie Bliss Como (chunky),
90% wool, 10% cashmere
(46yd/42m per 50g ball)
Small: 3 balls shade 06
Large: 6 balls shade 05
A pair of 7.5mm (US11:UK1) needles
7.5mm (US11:UK1) circular needle
Cable needle

FINISHED SIZE
Before felting (approx.)
Large container: 10in (26cm) diameter,
8in (20cm) high
Small container: 8in (20cm) diameter,
6in (15cm) high
After felting (approx.)
Large container: 8in (20cm) diameter,
6in (15cm) high
Small container: 5in (13cm) diameter,
4in (10cm) high

TENSION
12 sts and 17 rows to 4in (10cm) over st st using
7.5mm needles before felting.

Alternatives

These will look good in any room.
Try using a 100% wool space-dyed
yarn, or leaving the handles off
for a different look.

CONTAINER

Using 7.5mm needles, cast on 5 sts.
Next row: Inc in each of next 2 sts, k1, inc in
each of next 2 sts (9 sts).
Next and every following alternate row:
P to end.
Row 1: (K1, m1) to last st, k1 (17 sts).
Row 3: (K2, m1) to last st, k1 (25 sts).
Row 5: (K3, m1) to last st, k1 (33 sts).
Row 7: (K4, m1) to last st, k1 (41 sts).

Small container only

Continue in this way increasing 8 sts on 3 foll
right-side rows (65 sts).
Change to the circular needle.
Next row: (P9, m1) to last 2 sts, p2 (72 sts).

Large container only

Continue in this way increasing 8 sts on 6 foll
right-side rows (89 sts).
Change to the circular needle.
Next row: (P11, m1) to last st, p this st together
with 1st st on circular needle (96 sts).

Both containers

Cont in rounds to form sides.
Next round: P to end to form edge of base.
Foundation round: P2[3], * inc in each of next
4[6] sts, p4[6]; rep from * to last 6[9] sts, inc in
each of next 4[6] sts, p2[3] (108[144] sts).
Rounds 1 and 2: P2[3], * k8[12], p4[6]; rep from *
to last 10[15] sts, k8[12], P2[3].
Round 3: P2[3], * C4[6]B, C4[6]F, P4[6]; rep from
* to last 10[15] sts, C4[6]B, C4[6]F, p2[3].
Rounds 4 to 6[8]: Rep rounds 1 and 2 once
[twice] and round 1 again.
These 6[8] rounds form the pattern and are
repeated throughout.
Work straight until sides are 5[7]in (13[18]cm)
from start of sides.
Next round: P to end.
Next round: K to end.
Rep the last 2 rounds once more.
Cast off knitwise.

HANDLES
(make 2)
Using 7.5mm needles, cast on 7[10] sts
and work in garter st for 6³/₄[9]in (17[23]cm).
Cast off.

FINISHING OFF
With WS facing, gather round cast-on sts
and pull up tightly. Join base seam. Attach
handles to inside top at equal distance from
each other. Felt the containers by following
instructions given on page 164.

Pebbles
draught excluder

Organic wool in cool neutrals is used for these simple-to-knit pebbles. They are strung together to help keep the chill out of your warm winter lounge – also bringing a fun coastal theme to the room.

YOU WILL NEED

Rico Organic Pure Chunky, 100% wool (87yd/80m per 50g ball)
1 ball each of:
Off White (shade 001) (A)
Beige (shade 002) (B)
Light Grey (shade 004) (C)
A pair of 5.5mm (US9:UK5) needles
Stuffing

FINISHED SIZES

Large pebble: 6in (15cm) long, $3\frac{1}{2}$in (9cm) high
Medium pebble: 5in (12.5cm) long, 3in (7cm) high
Small pebble: 4in (10cm) long, 2in (5cm) high
To fit average doorway: 31in (80 cm).
Seven pebbles made.

TENSION

14 sts and 19 rows to 4in (10cm) over st st using 5.5mm needles.

LARGE PEBBLE
(make 1 in B)
Using 5.5mm needles cast on 3 sts.
Row 1: Inc knitwise in every st (6 sts).
Row 2 and every following alternate row:
P to end.
Row 3: Inc knitwise in every st (12 sts).
Row 5: (K1, inc in next st) to end (18 sts).
Row 7: (K2, inc in next st) to end (24 sts) **.
Continue increasing in this way to 42 sts.
Starting with a purl row, work 9 rows st st.
Row 23: (K5, k2tog) to end (36 sts).
Row 24 and every following alternate row:
P to end.
Row 25: (K4, k2tog) to end (30 sts).
Continue decreasing in this way to 12 sts,
ending with a purl row.
Next row: (K2tog) to end (6 sts).
Cast off.

MEDIUM PEBBLE
(make 3 in C, 1 in A and 1 in B)
Work as given for large pebble to **.
Continue increasing in this way to 36 sts.
Starting with a purl row, work 7 rows st st.
Row 19: (K4 sts, k2tog) to end (30 sts).
Row 20 and every following alternate row:
P to end.
Row 21: (K3, k2tog) to end (24 sts).
Continue decreasing in this way to 12 sts,
ending with a purl row.
Next row: K2tog to end (6 sts).
Cast off.

Alternatives

This draught excluder can be made to any
length. Or, a few loose pebbles in a bowl
would make an unusual decorative feature.

SMALL PEBBLE
(make 1 in A)
Cast on 10 sts.
Beg with a k row work 2 rows in st st.
Row 1: (K1, inc in next st) to end (15 sts).
Row 2 and every following alternate row:
P to end.
Row 3: (K2, inc in next st) to end (20 sts).
Row 5: (K3, inc in next st) to end (25 sts).
Starting with a purl row, st st for 9 rows.
Row 15: (K3, k2tog) to end (20 sts).
Row 16 and every following alternate row:
P to end.
Row 17: (K2, k2tog) to end (15 sts).
Row 19: (K1, k2tog) to end (10 sts).
Starting with a purl row, work 3 rows st st.
Cast off.

FINISHING OFF
Leaving a gap for stuffing, sew up seam of each
pebble. Stuff firmly. Tack together at ends to
form a line, pulling pebbles close together.

Dining room

THE DEEP **RICH** COLOURS OF **AUTUMN BERRIES** AND **WINTER FLOWERS** FORM THE PALETTE FOR THIS ROOM, BRINGING A TOUCH OF **WARMTH** AND **COZINESS** TO CHILLY EVENINGS. DINE IN STYLISH **COMFORT** WITH THESE **GORGEOUS** ACCESSORIES FOR YOUR TABLE.

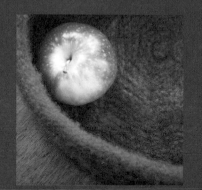

Berries felted fruit bowl

Textured place mats & coasters

Poinsettia napkin holders

Berries
felted fruit bowl

Space-dyed wool in rich berry tones is used to make this simple garter-stitch bowl. The felting adds an extra firmness to the bowl and gives the colours a soft blurred look whilst also adding a feeling of warmth.

YOU WILL NEED
Noro Kureyon (Aran), 100% wool
(110yd/101m per 50g ball)
5 balls shade 124
A pair of 6mm (US10:UK4) needles
6mm (US10:UK4) circular needle

PATTERN NOTES
Yarn is used double throughout. When knitting the base, it may be easier to use the circular needle after about six increase rows to prevent the knitting becoming too tight. Remember to continue to work in rows until all increases have been worked.

FINISHED SIZE
Before felting (approx.)
10in (25cm) diameter, 4in (11cm) high
After felting (approx.)
8in (20cm) diameter, 3½in (9cm) high

TENSION
14 sts and 20 rows to 4in (10cm) over st st using 6mm needles and with yarn used double before felting.

Alternatives
This bowl can be made to any size.
You could try using solid colours, or
higher sides for storage in other rooms.

FRUIT BOWL

Using 6mm needles, cast on 5 sts.
Next row: Inc in each of next 2 sts, k1, inc
in each of next 2 sts (9 sts).
Next and every following alternate row:
K to end.
Row 1: (K1, m1) to last st, k1 (17 sts).
Row 3: (K2, m1) to last st, k1 (25 sts).
Row 5: (K3, m1) to last st, k1 (33 sts).
Row 7: (K4, m1) to last st, k1 (41 sts).
Continue in this way increasing 8 sts on 10 foll
right-side rows (121 sts).
Change to circular needle.
Next row: K to last st on left-hand needle. Place
a marker here to indicate end of rounds, k last st
tog with next st on left-hand needle (120 sts).
Work in rounds as follows:

Round 1: P to end to form edge of base.
Round 2: K to end.
Rounds 3–9: Repeat rounds 1 and 2 three times
and round 1 again.
Round 10: K15, (m1, k30) 3 times, m1, k15 (124 sts).
Rounds 11–23: Repeat rounds 1 and 2 six times,
and round 1 again.
Round 24: K16, (m1, k31) 3 times, m1, k15 (128 sts).
Rounds 25–37: Repeat rounds 1 and 2 six times,
and round 1 again.
Round 38: K16, (m1, k32) 3 times, m1, k16 (132 sts).
Rounds 39–47: Repeat rounds 1 and 2 four
times, and round 1 again.
Rounds 48–53: K to end.
Cast off loosely.

FINISHING OFF

With wrong side facing, gather round cast-on sts
and pull up tightly. Join base seam. Felt the bowl
by following instructions given on page 164.

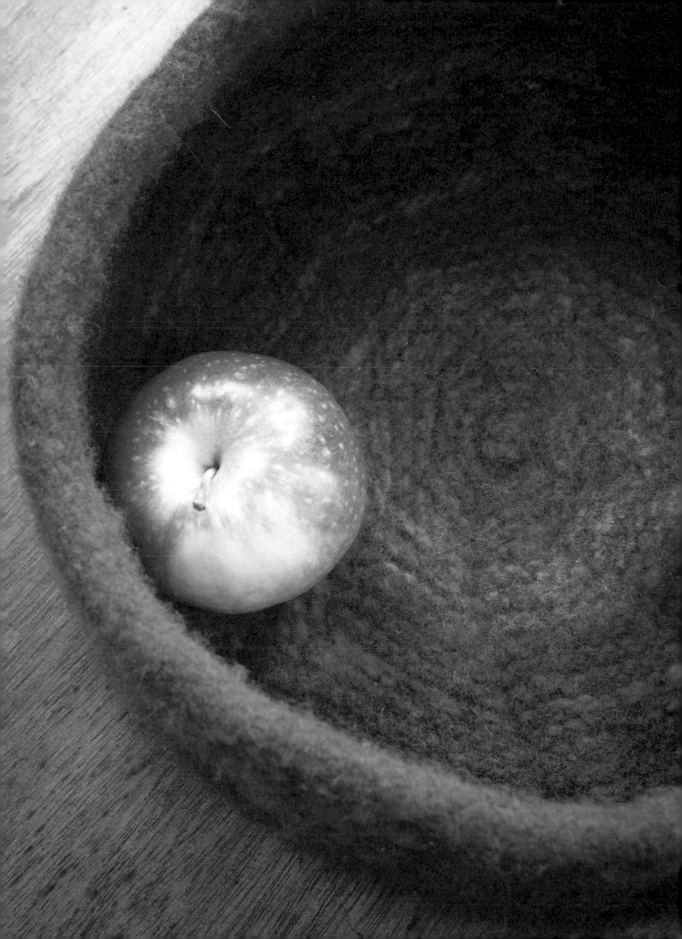

Textured
place mats & coasters

These place mats and coasters use a simple twist texture stitch in stone and grape mercerized cotton to produce a classic table set. The rich colours will make a stylish but relaxed statement for your dining table.

YOU WILL NEED

Patons 100% Cotton DK
(230yd/210m per 100g ball)
5 balls Limestone (shade 716) (A)
2 balls Grape (shade 733) (B)
(These are the yarn quantities for 4 sets)
A pair each of 3mm (US2:UK11) and 3.25mm
(US3:UK10) needles
2mm (USB/1:UK14) crochet hook

FINISHED SIZE

Place mats: 17$\frac{1}{4}$in (44cm) wide x 13$\frac{1}{2}$in
(34cm) deep
Coasters: 4$\frac{3}{4}$in (12cm) x 4$\frac{3}{4}$in (12cm)

TENSION

32 sts and 33 rows to 4in (10cm) over pattern
using 3.25mm needles.

PATTERN NOTE

When working the edging, do not work
the dc too close together, as this will
cause the edges to frill.

Alternatives

These mats and coasters can be made to any size. The place mat can be continued in a long strip to make a table runner. Add different coloured edgings or other simple textures to vary the look.

PLACE MAT

Using 3mm needles and A, cast on 118 sts.

Row 1: (RS) P to end.

Row 2: K to end.

Change to 3.25mm needles.

Cont in patt.

Rows 1 and 3: P2, (k2, p2) to end.

Rows 2 and 4: K2, (p2, k2) to end.

Row 5: P2, (TW2l, p2) to end.

Rows 6, 8 and 10: K4, (p2, k2) to last 6 sts, p2, k4.

Rows 7 and 9: P4, (k2, p2) to last 6 sts, k2, p4.

Row 11: P4, (TW2l, p2) to last 6 sts, TW2l, p4.

Row 12: K2, (p2, k2) to end.

These 12 rows form the pattern.

Rows 13 to 96: Work rows 1 to 12 seven times.

Row 97: As row 1.

Row 98: As row 2.

Row 99: As row 5.

Next row: K to end.

Next row: P to end.

Cast off knitwise.

COASTERS

Using 3.25mm needles and A, cast on 30 sts.

Row 1: (RS) K to end.

Change to 3.25mm needles.

Cont in patt as given for place mat.

Rows 1 to 24: Work rows 1 to 12 twice.

Row 25: As row 1.

Row 26: As row 2.

Row 27: As row 5.

Next row: K to end.

Cast off purlwise.

CROCHET EDGING FOR BOTH

Using 2mm crochet hook and B, with RS of mat or coaster facing, starting along any side, work the following:

Row 1: Sl st into main fabric, 1ch, work 1 round of dcs evenly around all edging with 3dc worked into each centre of each corner, sl st into 1st dc of row, 1ch, turn.

Row 2: work 1dc into each dc, working 3dc into centre of each corner, sl st into 1st dc of row, 1ch, turn.

Repeat row 2 once more.

Fasten off.

FINISHING OFF

Press according to ball band instructions.

Poinsettia napkin holders

Winter poinsettia flowers form the motif for the napkin holders, using rich, strong colours in a soft alpaca yarn. Beads at the centre of the flowers add delicate detailing that will catch the light at a candle-lit dinner party.

YOU WILL NEED

Alpaca Select 100% Alpaca DK
(115yd/105m per 50g ball)
Amounts are given for 4 napkin rings
1 ball shade 17 (A)
4 balls shade 36 (B)
1 ball shade 23 (C)
3mm (USD/3:UK10) and 3.5mm (USE/4:UK9)
crochet hook
Small glass beads

FINISHED SIZES

Flower: approx. $4^{1}/_{4}$in (11cm)
Band: approx. 8in (20cm) round

TENSION

Tension is not critical for this project.

PATTERN NOTE

Yarn is used double for the band, and singly for the flowers and leaves.

BAND

Using 3.5mm hook and B double, make a chain of 34, sl st into 1st ch to form a ring, 1ch, 1dc into each ch to end, sl st into 1st dc of ring, 1ch, turn (34 dc).

Round 1: 1dc into each dc to end, sl st into 1st dc of round, 1ch, turn.

Round 2: 1dc in each of next 2dc, (work dc2tog, 1dc in each of next 6dc) to end.

Repeat round 1 until band measures 6cm, ending on a WS round.

Fasten off.

FLOWER
(Make 6 petals per flower)

Using 3mm hook and A singly, make 4ch.

Row 1: 1dc into 2nd ch from hook, 1dc into each of next 2ch, turn (3 dc).

Row 2: 1ch, 1dc into each dc, turn.

Row 3: 1ch, 1dc into 1st dc, 3dc into next dc, 1dc into last dc, turn (5 dc).

Row 4: 1ch, 1dc into each dc, turn.

Rows 5–8: As row 4.

Row 9: 1ch, work dc2tog over first 2dc, 1dc into next dc, work dc2tog over last 2dc, turn (3 dc).

Rows 10–11: 1ch, 1dc into each dc, turn.

Row 12: Miss first dc, work dc2tog over last 2dc (pulling through all 3 loops remaining on hook).

Fasten off.

CENTRE

Using 3mm hook and B singly, make a circle by wrapping yarn around your finger, remove and hold with the thumbnail and forefinger, place hook through loop and draw through the yarn to make a sl st. Work 6dc into loop, sl st into 1st dc of round. Pull yarn tight to form a small circle, turn.

Round 2: 1ch, 2dc into each dc, sl st into 1st dc of round.

Fasten off, leaving a long length.

LEAVES
(make 3 per napkin ring)

Using 3mm hook and C singly, make 13ch, 1dc into 2nd ch from hook, 1dc into next ch, 1htr into next ch, leaving the last loop of each on hook, work 1tr into each of next 2ch, yrh, and draw through all loops (cluster made), 2dtr cluster over next 2ch, 1dtr into each of next 4ch, 1tr into next ch, 2ch, sl st into same place as last tr, 2ch, work opposite side of ch, 1tr into same place as ss, 1dtr into each of next 4ch, 2dtr cluster over next 2ch, 1tr cluster over next 2ch, 1htr into next ch, 1dc into each of last 2ch, sl st into 1st dc of leaf. Fasten off.

FINISHING OFF

Overlap each petal with previous petal to form a flower shape, sew in place. Sew centre to centre of flower. Place the three leaves behind the flower allowing the leaves to show behind the petals. Sew into place. Place this centrally on the napkin band and sew into place. Sew beads onto centre of each flower.

Alternatives

Once the base is made, any motifs can be added. Try leaves with beads for berries for a winter alternative. Using different flowers and yarns can make a set for each season. Wooden beads or sequins will give them a different look.

Kitchen

THE KITCHEN IS THE **WARM** AND **WELCOMING** **HEART** OF A HOME AND DESERVES **BEAUTIFUL** HOMEMADE ACCESSORIES. OVERFLOWING BASKETS OF **FLOWERS** FRESH FROM THE **MARKET** ARE THE INSPIRATION FOR THIS ROOM.

Flower

Pansies shopper

English rose tea cozy

Basket-stitch mug cozies

Pansies shopper

A basket for market shopping inspired the base for this bag, with colourful pansies along the top in matt and mercerized cotton. A pretty contrasting lining in cotton gingham adds a fresh country look.

YOU WILL NEED
Rico Creative Cotton Aran, 100% cotton
(93yd/85m per 50g ball)
6 balls Clay (shade 51) (A) (used double)
Rico Cotton Essentials DK, 100% cotton
(142yd/130m per 50g ball)
1 ball each of:
Cream (shade 51) (B)
Purple (shade 18) (C)
Patons 100% Cotton DK
(230yd/210m per 100g ball)
1 ball Moss (shade 1) (D)
Small amount black embroidery cotton
A pair each of 3mm (US2:UK11) and 5mm
(US8:UK6) needles
Piece of lining fabric: 16 x 24in (40 x 60cm)

FINISHED SIZE
14in (35cm) wide x 12in (30cm) deep

TENSION
17 sts and 23 rows to 4in (10cm) over st st using
5mm needles and 2 strands of A.

BAG
(made in one piece)

Using 5mm needles and 2 strands of A, cast on 56 sts.

Row 1: * K7, (p1, k1) 3 times, p1; rep from * to end.

Row 2: * K1, (p1, k1) 3 times, p7; rep from * to end.

Row 3: * P8, (k1, p1) 3 times; rep from * to end.

Row 4: As row 2.

Row 5: As row 1.

Row 6: * (K1, p1) 3 times, k8; rep from * to end.

Rows 7 and 8: As rows 1 and 2.

Row 9: As row 3.

Row 10: As row 2.

Row 11: As row 1.

Row 12: * P7, k1, (p1, k1) 3 times; rep from * to end.

Row 13: * P1, (k1, p1) 3 times, k7; rep from * to end.

Row 14: * K8, (p1, k1) 3 times; rep from * to end.

Row 15: As row 13.

Row 16: As row 12.

Row 17: * (P1, k1) 3 times, p8; rep from * to end.

Row 18: As row 12.

Row 19: As row 13.

Row 20: As row 14.

Row 21: As row 13.

Row 22: As row 12.

These 22 rows form the pattern.

Cont in patt until work measures approx 24in (60cm) from cast-on edge, ending with a row 22. Cast off.

HANDLES
(make 2)

Using 5mm needles and 2 strands of A, cast on 10 sts.

Work in garter st, until handle measures 12in (30cm).

Cast off.

PANSIES
(make 10)

Yarn is used singly throughout.

Top front petals
(make 2 per flower)

Using 3mm needles and B, cast on 9 sts.

Row 1: Knit.

Row 2: P1, m1, p7, m1, p1 (11 sts).

Row 3: K1, m1, k9, m1, k1 (13 sts).

Row 4: P to end.

Join in C.

Row 5: K5B, 3C, 5B.

Row 6: P4B, 5C, 4B.

Row 7: K3B, 7C, 3B.

Row 8: Using B, p2tog, p2B, 5C, 2B, using B, p2tog, tbl.

Row 9: Using B, skpo, k2B, 3C, 2B, using B, k2tog.

Row 10: Using B, p2tog, p1B, 3C, 1B, using B, p2tog tbl (7 sts).

Leave sts on a holder.

Lower front petal
(make 1 per flower)

Using 3mm needles and B, cast on 11 sts.

Row 1: Knit.

Row 2: P1, m1, p9, m1, p1 (13 sts).

Row 3: K1, m1, k11, m1, k1 (15 sts).

Row 4: P1, m1, p13, m1, p1 (17 sts).

Join in C.

Row 5: K4B, 9C, 4B.

Row 6: P3B, 11C, 3B.

Row 7: Using B, skpo, k2B, 9C, using B, k2, k2tog.

Row 8: Using B, p2tog, P2B, 7C, using B, p2, p2tog, tbl.

Row 9: Using B, skpo, k2B, 5C, using B, k2, k2tog.

Row 10: Using B, p2tog, P2B, 3C, using B, p2, p2tog, tbl (9 sts).

Leave sts on holder.

Back top petals
(make 2)

Using 3mm needles and C, cast on 9 sts.

Row 1: Knit.

Row 2: P1, m1, p7, m1, p1 (11 sts).

Row 3: K1, m1, k9, m1, k1 (13 sts).

Row 4: P to end.

Row 5: K to end.

Rows 6–9: Rep rows 4 and 5 twice more.

Row 10: P2tog, p to last 2 sts, p2tog tbl.

Row 11: Skpo, k to last 2 sts, k2tog.

Row 12: As row 10 (9 sts).

Leave sts on holder.

LEAVES
(make 2 per flower)

Using 3mm needles and D, cast on 3 sts.

Foundation row: K1, p1, k1.

Row 1: K1, m1, k1, m1, k1 (5 sts).

Row 2: K2, p1, k2.

Row 3: K2, m1, k1, m1, k2 (7 sts).

Rows 4, 6, 8, 10, 12, 14 and 16: Knit to centre st, p1, knit to end.

Row 5: K3, m1, k1, m1, k3 (9 sts).

Row 7: Knit to end.

Row 9: As row 7.

Row 11: Skpo, k5, k2tog (7 sts).

Row 13: Knit to end.

Row 15: Skpo, k3, k2tog (5 sts).

Row 17: Skpo, k1, k2tog (3 sts).

Row 18: Sl1, k2tog, psso.

Fasten off.

FINISHING OFF

Using knitted piece as a template, allowing ³⁄₄in (2cm) seam allowance, cut out lining. Join side seams. Turn seam allowance to wrong side along top edge. Join sides of bag. With wrong sides together, place lining inside bag and slip stitch in place.

Using a length of embroidery cotton, and a tapestry needle, thread through sts of 2 top front petals and one lower front petal left on holders, repeat once more, pull yarn together tightly, secure, do not fasten off.

Use embroidery cotton to oversew randomly in the centre of the petals to form a small mound and stamen. Fasten off.

With the two top back petals and C, thread through sts left on holder, rep once more, pull the yarn together, secure, place behind the top front petals overlapping them slightly, sew in place.

Place two leaves behind each flower and sew five flowers to each front and back. Finally, sew on the handles.

Alternatives

Try using different flowers on the top for an alternative look, such as the poinsettia from the napkin holders (pattern on page 34).

English rose
tea cozy

Soft alpaca yarn in a simple textured stitch forms the base of this gorgeous tea cozy. A sweet bunch of roses and dainty leaves on top make this a perfect centrepiece for a delicious afternoon tea.

YOU WILL NEED

Artesano Aran, 50% alpaca, 50% wool, (144yd/132m per 100g hank)
1 hank Pine (shade C853) (A)
Artesano Alpaca DK, 100% alpaca (109yd/100m per 50g ball)
1 ball each of:
Sweet Pea (shade CA13) (B)
Violet (shade CA704) (C)
Fern (shade CA743) (D)
A pair each of 3.25mm (US3:UK10), 4mm (US6:UK8) and 5mm (US8:UK6) needles

FINISHED SIZE

To fit medium-sized teapot
9in (23cm) wide at bottom x 7in (18cm) deep

TENSION

17 sts and 30 rows to 4in (10cm) over pattern using 5mm needles.

SIDES

(make 2)

Using 5mm needles and A, cast on 39 sts.

Next row: P to end.

Next row: K to end.

Cont in pattern.

Row 1 and every following alt row: (RS) K to end.

Rows 2 and 4: K3, (p1, k3) to end.

Rows 6 and 8: K1, (p1, k3) to last 2 sts, p1, k1.

These 8 rows form the pattern.

Continue until work measures 6in (15cm), ending with row 4 of pattern.

Shape top

Keeping pattern correct, work as follows:

Row 1: K8, (skpo) 4 times, k to last 16 sts, (k2tog) 4 times, k8 (31 sts).

Row 2: K1, (p1, k3) to last 2 sts, p1, k1.

Row 3: K to end.

Row 4: As row 2.

Row 5: K4, (skpo) 4 times, k to last 12 sts, (k2tog) 4 times, k4 (23 sts).

Row 6: (K3, p1) to last 3 sts, k3.

Row 7: K to end.

Row 8: As row 6.

Row 9: (Skpo) 4 times, k to last 8 sts (k2tog) 4 times (15 sts).

Row 10: As row 2.

Row 11: K to end.

Row 12: (K2tog) 3 times, k3 (k2tog tbl) 3 times.

Cast off knitwise.

ROSES

(make 3 in each of B and C)

A two-tone flower can be made by using the contrast colour for rows 5 and 6 and the cast-off row.

Using 3.25mm needles cast on 11 sts.

Row 1: K to end.

Row 2: P into front and back of first st, (p1, p into front and back of next st) to end (17 sts).

Row 3: K to end.

Row 4: (P into front and back of next st) 6 times, p5, (p into front and back of next st) 6 times (29 sts).

Row 5: K to end.

Row 6: P to end.

Cast-off row: K1, (leaving st on left-hand needle, k into front of next st, cast off this st, then k into back of st, taking it off the needle, cast off this st), to last st, cast off this st.

LEAVES

(make 7)

Using 4mm needles and D, cast on 3 sts.

Foundation row: K1, p1, k1.

Row 1: K1, m1, k1, m1, k1 (5 sts).

Row 2: K2, p1, k2.

Row 3: K2, m1, k1, m1, k2 (7 sts).

Rows 4, 6, 8, 10, 12: K to centre st, p1, k to end.

Row 5: K3, m1, k1, m1, k3 (9 sts).

Row 7: K4, m1, k1, m1, k4 (11 sts).

Row 9: Skpo, k7, k2tog (9 sts).

Row 11: Skpo, k5, k2tog (7 sts).

Row 13: Skpo, k3, skpo (5 sts).

Row 14: K to end.

Row 15: Skpo, k1, k2tog (3 sts).

Row 16: Sl1, k2tog, psso.

Fasten off.

FINISHING OFF

Sew side seams, allowing gaps of $3\frac{1}{2}$in (9cm) for the spout and 4in (10cm) for the handle.

With st st facing outwards, roll roses into a bud shape. Using yarn from cast-on edge, thread through the bud and secure.

Arrange leaves around centre top of cozy and sew in place. Place roses to form a group on top of leaves and sew in place.

Basket-stitch mug cozies

These mug cozies in soft alpaca use a simple basket stitch in knit and purl, with a colourful contrast border. They are quick to knit, and will keep your hands, as well as your tea, warm on chilly days.

YOU WILL NEED
Artesano Alpaca Aran, 50% alpaca, 50% wool (144yd/132m per 100g hank)
1 hank Ash (shade C969) (A)
Artesano Alpaca DK, 100% alpaca (109yd/100m per 50g ball)
1 ball Violet (shade CA704) (B)
(note: this yarn is used double)
A pair of 5.5mm (US9:UK5) needles
1 button per cozy approx. ¾in (1.5cm) diameter

FINISHED SIZES
Approx. 9in (22cm) circumference

TENSION
15 sts and 23 rows to 4in (10cm) over pattern using 5.5mm needles.

MUG COZY

Using 5.5mm needles and B used double, cast on 37 sts.

Knit 2 rows.

Break off B.

Join in A.

Next row: Inc in first st, p to last st, inc in last st (39 sts).

Cont in patt.

Row 1: K7, (p5, k5) to last 2 sts, k2.

Row 2: K2, p5, (k5, p5) to last 2 sts, k2.

Rows 3, 5, 6 and 8: As row 1.

Rows 4, 7 and 9: As row 2.

Row 10: K7, (p5, k5) to last 2 sts, k2.

Rows 11–15: As rows 1–5.

Next row: P2tog, p to last 2 sts, p2tog.

Break off A.

With B used double, cast on 4 sts, k these 4 sts, then k to end.

Next row: K to last 4 sts, k1, yf, k2tog, k1.

Next row: K to end.

Cast off.

FINISHING OFF

Join border at cast-on edge.

Attach button to top.

Alternatives

You could also knit the mug cozy with deeper dimensions to fit a cafetière. Any simple stitch can be used – try fresh stripes for a summer look.

Garden

FRESHLY POTTED **PLANTS** AND **IDYLLIC**
COUNTRYSIDE VIEWS ARE THE THEME FOR THE
GARDEN; A **CALM** AND **PEACEFUL** PLACE TO
RELAX IN WITH TONES OF **INVIGORATING** GREEN.

Down to

Ploughed fields patchwork throw

Grain & ridge plant pot holders

Large leaf cushion cover

earth

Ploughed fields
patchwork throw

The random patchwork of green fields inspire the design for this throw. A beautiful country tweed yarn used in a striking ridged rib stitch gives the hexagons the look of freshly ploughed earth.

YOU WILL NEED

Debbie Bliss Donegal Luxury Tweed Aran,
85% wool, 15% angora
(96yd/88m per 50g ball)
5 balls each of:
shade 10 (A)
shade 08 (B)
shade 11 (C)
A pair of 5mm (US8:UK6) needles

FINISHED SIZE

Approx. 42$\frac{1}{2}$in (108cm) x 53in (135cm)

TENSION

18 sts and 24 rows to 4in (10cm) over st st using 5mm needles.

PATTERN NOTE

The motifs here are sewn together in different directions. A more regular look can be achieved by keeping the stitches going in one direction.

MOTIF
(make 8 in each colour)
Using 5mm needles cast on 27 sts.
Pattern row: (RS) K2, (p2, k2) to last st, p1.
This row forms the patt and is repeated.
Row 2: Inc in first st, k1, (p2, k2) to last st,
inc in last st.
Row 3: P1, (k2, p2) to end.
Keeping continuity of pattern, and bringing
extra sts into pattern, inc 1 st at each end of
next row and every following wrong-side row
until 15 inc rows have been worked (57 sts).
Pattern 1 row straight.
Next row: Skpo, p1, (k2, p2) to last 2 sts, k2tog.
Next row: (P2, k2) to last 3 sts, p2, k1.
Next row: Skpo, (k2, p2) to last 5 sts, k2, p1,
k2tog.
Next row: P1, (k2, p2) to end.
Keeping continuity of pattern, continue to
dec 1 st each end of next and every following
wrong-side row until 15 dec rows have been
worked (27 sts).
Work 1 row straight.
Cast off.

FINISHING OFF
Pin together to form throw, alternating colours.
This throw has been put together by changing
the direction of the knitting (see assembly
diagram opposite), but it can be assembled
with the knitting in the normal direction for a
more regular look. Using a contrast colour work
in blanket stitch around the outside edge.

Alternatives
As the throw is made up of separate motifs,
it can be made to any size. Try subtle
neutrals or brights for a very different look.
A single motif can be used as a mat to put
under your plant pots.

ASSEMBLY DIAGRAM

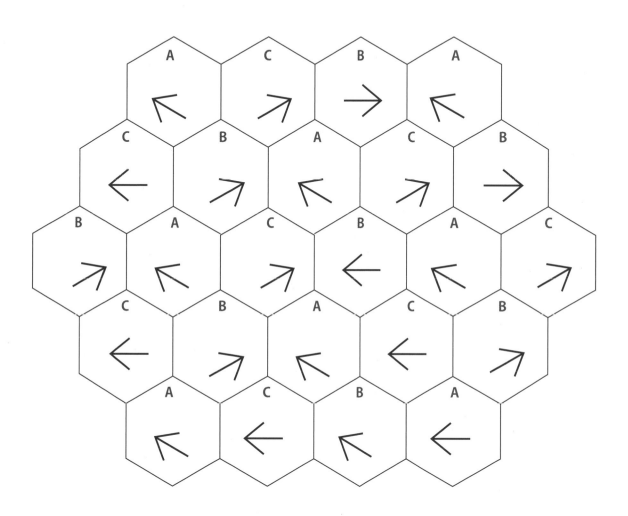

Key to diagram

A Shade 10
B Shade 08
C Shade 11
⤢ Direction of knitting

Grain & ridge
plant pot holders

A fresh green cotton yarn is used for these plant pot holders, using ridge and bobble crochet stitches. They have a fun, textured look, creating tactile colourful containers that can be dotted around your garden.

YOU WILL NEED

Debbie Bliss Eco Aran Fairtrade Collection, 100% cotton (82yd/75m per 50g ball)
Large: 3 balls shade 620
Medium: 2 balls shade 620
Small: 1 ball shade 620
3.5mm (USE/4:UK 9) and 4mm (USG/6:UK 8) crochet hooks

PATTERN NOTE

These can be made to any size. Work the base to the size of your plant pot base then work the sides.

FINISHED SIZE

Large: To fit base: $4^{1}/_{2}$in (11cm) diameter, height $6^{3}/_{4}$in (17cm)
Medium: To fit base: 4in (10cm) diameter, height $5^{1}/_{2}$in (14cm)
Small: To fit base: $2^{3}/_{4}$in (7cm) diameter, height $3^{1}/_{2}$in (9cm)
These can be made to any size by working more or fewer rows on base and sides.

TENSION

16 sts and 16 rows to 4in (10cm) over main pattern using 4mm hook.

SPECIAL ABBREVIATION

Pdc – picot double crochet: insert hook into st being worked, wrap yarn and draw through, (wrap yarn and draw through loop) 3 times so that 3ch are made, wrap yarn and draw through both loops on hook (pdc made). Keep loops to front (RS) of fabric.

PLANT POT HOLDER
Foundation round

Make a circle by wrapping yarn around forefinger, take loop off finger but still hold it between thumb and forefinger, insert hook through loop, yrh, draw through circle, yrh, draw through loop (ss made).

Using 4mm hook, work 6dc, pull the loose end firmly to close the circle, ss into 1st dc of round, weave the end in WS of work.

All sizes

Round 1: 1ch, (2dc into next dc) to end ss into top of 1st dc of round (12 dc).

Round 2: 1ch, 1dc into each dc, ss into top of 1st dc of round.

Round 3: 1ch, (2dc into next dc) to end ss into top of 1st dc of round (24 dc).

Round 4: 1ch, 1dc into each dc, ss into top of 1st dc of round.

Medium and large size only

Round 5: 1ch, (2dc into next dc, 1dc in next dc) to end ss into top of 1st dc of round (36 dc).

Round 6: 1ch, 1dc into each dc, ss into top of 1st dc of round.

Round 7: 1ch, (2dc into next dc, 1dc in each of next 2dc) to end ss into top of 1st dc of round (48 dc).

Large size only

Round 8: 1ch, 1dc into each dc, ss into top of 1st dc of round.

Round 9: 1ch, (2dc into next dc, 1dc in each of next 3dc) to end ss into top of 1st dc of round (60 dc).

SIDES
All sizes

Special note: corded dc – this creates decorative ridge A.

Change to 3.5mm hook.

Now work in rows, working back and forth and working ss into 1st st of each row to form a round.

Row 1: (RS) (Work into back loops only of previous round), 3ch (count as 1tr), 1tr into each dc to end, ss onto top of 3ch at beg of row, do not turn.

Row 2: 1ch, work from left to right and working into front loops only, start with the hook facing downwards, (insert the hook back into the next st to the right, pull the yarn through, twisting the hook to face upwards at the same time, wrap the yarn and draw through to work the dc as normal) to end, ss in 1ch.

Row 3: 3ch (counts as 1st tr) working into back loops of previous tr row, 1tr into each tr to end, do not turn, ss into top of 3ch at beg of row.

Small size only

Rep rows 2 and 3 twice more, then row 2 again. Place 4 markers evenly around top of last tr row.

Next row: 3ch (counts as 1st tr) working into back loops of previous tr row, (1tr into each tr to marker, 2 tr in marked tr) 4 times, 1tr in each tr to end, do not turn, ss into top of 3ch at beg of row (28 tr).

Rep rows 2 and 3 once more, inc 2 tr evenly on last row (30 tr).

Medium size only

Rep rows 2 and 3 four times more, then row 2 again.

Place 6 markers evenly around top of last tr row.

Next row: 3ch (counts as 1st tr) working into back loops of previous tr row, (1tr into each tr to marker, 2tr in marked tr) 6 times, 1tr in each tr to end, do not turn, ss into top of 3ch at beg of row (54 tr).

Rep rows 2 and 3 four times more.

Large size only

Rep rows 2 and 3 six times more, then row 2 again.

Place 8 markers evenly around top of last tr row.

Next row: 3ch (counts as 1st tr) working into back loops of previous tr row, (1tr into each tr to marker, 2tr in marked tr) 8 times, 1tr in each tr to end, do not turn, ss into top of 3ch at beg of row (68 tr).

Rep rows 2 and 3 four times more, inc 2tr evenly on last row (70 tr).

Alternatives

Mix and match the colours used for the holders and use with empty plant pots for attractive storage in any room.

GRANITE STITCH FOLD-OVER RIDGE
All sizes

Round 1: 1ch, 1dc into 3ch of previous round, 1dc into each tr, ss 1st dc of round.

Turn work so that each following round is worked on WS of work, which will be RS when folded over.

Round 2: 1ch, 1dc into each dc, ss into top of 1st dc of round.

Repeat round 2 1[3:5] times more.

Now work in granule patt.

Round 1: 1ch, 1dc into 1st dc, (1pdc into next dc, 1dc into next dc) to last dc, 1pdc into last dc, ss into 1st dc of round, do not turn.

Round 2: 1ch, 1dc into 1st dc, 1dc into each st where pdc was made (hold the pdc down and you will see the loops of the pdc) and each dc, ss into 1st dc of round, do not turn.

Round 3: 1ch, 1pdc into first dc, (1dc into next dc, 1pdc into next dc) to last dc, 1dc into last dc, ss into 1st dc of round, do not turn.

Round 4: As round 2.

Medium size only

Repeat rounds 1 and 2 once more.

Large size only

Repeat rounds 1 to 4, then rounds 1 and 2 again.

All sizes

Fasten off.

FINISHING OFF

Sew in ends.

Fold granule ridge over to form a rim.

Large leaf cushion cover

A soft merino cashmere silk mix yarn is used for this cushion cover. A simple, oversized intarsia leaf motif in a colourful green makes it a fresh and striking addition to your favourite garden chair.

YOU WILL NEED

Sublime Cashmere Merino Silk Aran,
75% extra fine merino, 20% silk, 5% cashmere
(94yd/86m per 50g ball)
6 balls Vanilla (shade 03) (A)
1 ball Sprout (shade 19) (B)
1 ball Mole (shade 56) (C)
Cushion pad 20 x 20in (51 x 51cm)
A pair of 5mm (US8:UK6) needles
5 buttons, approx. 1in (2cm) diameter

FINISHED SIZE

20 x 20in (51 x 51cm)

TENSION

18 sts and 24 rows to 4in (10cm) over st st using 5mm needles.

PATTERN NOTES

When working from chart, right-side rows are knit rows and read from right to left. Wrong-side rows are purl rows and read from left to right. Use separate balls of yarn for each area of colour and twist yarns on wrong side to avoid a hole when changing colour.

Large leaf cushion cover chart
(72 sts x 93 rows)

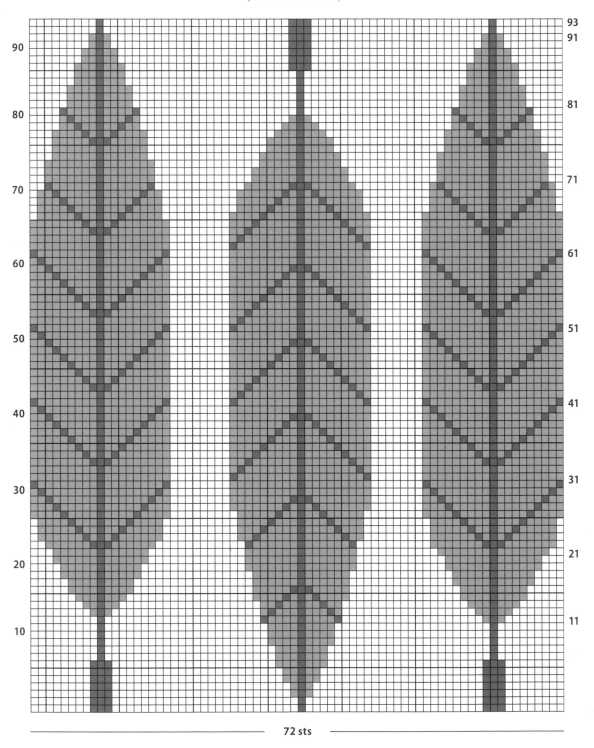

72 sts

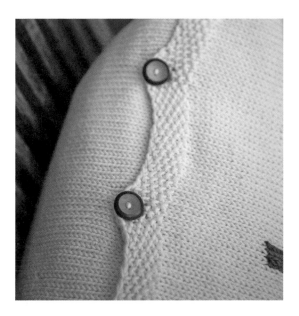

Key to chart

☐ **A** Vanilla
▨ **B** Sprout
▧ **C** Mole

1 square represents 1 stitch and 1 row

CUSHION COVER

Knitted in one piece starting at top back.

Back

Using 5mm needles and A, cast on 92 sts.
Beg with a k row work in st st for 120 rows.
Mark each end of last row with a coloured
thread.

Front

Work a further 14 rows.
Work in patt from chart.
Row 1: K10A, patt across 72 sts of row 1
of chart, k10A.
Row 2: P10A, patt across 72 sts of row 2
of chart, p10A.
Cont in this way until all 93 rows have been
worked.
Cont in A only.
Work 13 rows.
Mark each end of last row with a coloured
thread.

Overlap and buttonhole band

Using A, work 6 rows in st st.
Moss st row 1: (K1, p1) to end.
Moss st row 2: (P1, k1) to end.
These 2 rows form the moss st.
Work 1 more row.
Buttonhole row: Moss st 3, (work 2tog, yrn,
moss st 19) 4 times, work 2tog, yrn, moss st 3.
Work 4 rows in moss st.
Cast off in moss st.

FINISHING OFF

Press sides according to yarn band instructions.
Using coloured threads to denote fold line,
sew side seams. Sew buttons on to top edge
to correspond with buttonholes.

Alternatives

Use more stitches around the motifs
for a floor cushion, or fewer around
one motif only for a smaller rectangular
cushion cover.

Main bedroom

RETRO-STYLE CIRCLES INSPIRE THE DESIGNS IN THIS ROOM. THE COLOUR PALETTE IS **SOFT** AND **RELAXING**: COFFEE, CREAM, PASTELS, WITH ADDED **TEXTURE** AND A **LUXURIOUS** FEEL.

Textured

Circle patches bedcover

Rosette cushion cover

Textured hot water bottle cover

circles

Circle patches bedcover

Merino cashmere silk mix yarn in neutrals and soft pastels is used for this bedcover. The circle intarsia motif in squares repeat in alternating colourways, giving this snuggly blanket a retro look.

YOU WILL NEED

Sublime Cashmere Merino Silk Aran,
75% extra fine merino, 20% silk, 5% cashmere
(94yd/86m per 50g ball)
11 balls Vanilla (shade 03) (A)
9 balls Fennel (shade 132) (B)
3 balls Bay (shade 135) (C)
1 ball Chicory (shade 127) (D)
A pair each of 4.5mm (US7:UK7) and 5mm
(US8:UK6) needles

FINISHED SIZE

42$\frac{1}{2}$in (108cm) deep x 54in (137cm) wide

TENSION

18 sts and 24 rows to 4ins (10cm) over st st
using 5mm needles.

PATTERN NOTES

When working from chart, right-side rows are knit rows and read from right to left. Wrong-side rows are purl rows and read from left to right. Use separate balls of yarn for each area of colour and twist yarn on wrong side to avoid a hole when changing colour.

Colourway 1: Cream base (A), Light Brown circle (B): make 8

Colourway 2: Light Brown base (B), Cream circle (A): make 8

Colourway 3: Cream base (A), Light Blue circle (C): make 7

Colourway 4: Light Brown base (B), Pale Green circle (D): make 7

CIRCLE PATCHES

Using 5mm needles and main colour of square, cast on 40 sts.

Knit 2 rows.

Next row: K2, patt across 36 sts of row 1 of chart, k2.

Next row: K2, patt across 36 sts of row 2 of chart, k2.

These 2 rows set the position of the pattern and form the garter st border.

Cont in this way until all 48 rows have been worked.

Knit 2 rows.

Cast off.

EDGING

Long sides

With 4.5mm needles and A, pick up and knit 236 sts.

** Row 1: K to end.

Row 2: K3, m1, k to last 3 sts, m1, k3.

Rep rows 1 and 2 once more and row 1 again.

Break off A.

Join in C.

Work rows 2 and 1.

Cast off **.

Short sides

With 4.5mm needles and A, pick up and knit 187 sts.

Work as given for long sides from ** to **.

FINISHING OFF

Join row ends of edgings to form mitred corners. Join pieces together, referring to the numbers on the diagram below that correspond with the colourway number shown above.

Key to chart

☐ Main colour
■ Contrast colour

1 square represents 1 stitch and 1 row

ASSEMBLY DIAGRAM

2	1	3	4	2	1
4	2	1	3	4	2
3	4	2	1	3	4
1	3	4	2	1	3
2	1	3	4	2	1

CIRCLE PATCH CHART
(36 sts x 48 rows)

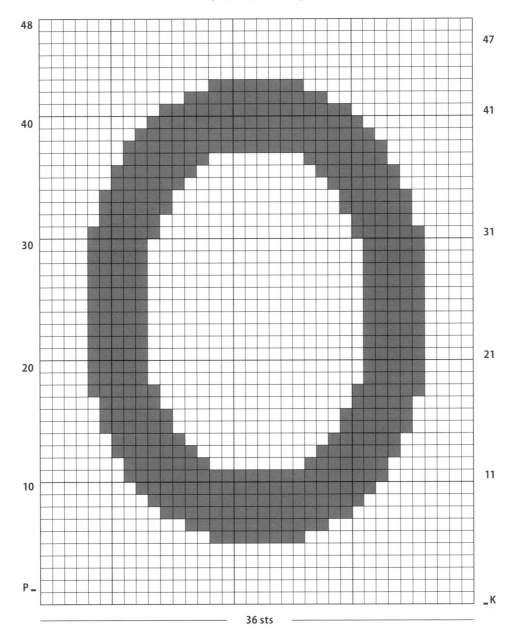

Rosette cushion cover

Soft merino yarns in coffee and cream are used for this tactile cushion cover. Deeply textured rosettes sit upon a simple intarsia circle motif, inviting you to lie back and relax.

YOU WILL NEED

Debbie Bliss Rialto Aran, 100% wool
(88yd/80m per 50g ball)
3 balls shade 25 (A)
3 balls shade 01 (B)
2 balls shade 16 (C)
A pair each of 4.5mm (US7:UK7) and 5mm
(US8:UK6) needles
Cushion pad 18 x 18in (45 x 45cm)

FINISHED SIZE

18 x 18in (45 x 45cm)

TENSION

18 sts and 24 rows to 4in (10cm) over st st using 5mm needles.

PATTERN NOTES

When working from chart, right-side rows are knit rows and read from right to left. Wrong-side rows are purl rows and read from left to right. Use separate balls of yarn for each area of colour and twist yarn on wrong side to avoid a hole when changing colour.

CUSHION COVER

Knitted in one piece starting at top back.

Back

Using 4.5mm needles and A cast on 81 sts.
Moss st row 1: K1, (p1, k1) to end.
This row forms the moss st.
Work 5 more rows.
Change to 5mm needles.
Beg with a knit row, work 80 rows in st st.
Mark each end of last row with a coloured thread.

Front

Work a further 20 rows st st.
Work in patt from chart.
Row 1: K15A, patt across 51 sts of row 1 of chart, k15A.
Row 2: P15A, patt across 51 sts of row 2 of chart, p15A.
These 2 rows set the position of the chart.
Keeping 15 sts in A at each side, continue to follow chart until 66 rows have been worked.
Continue in A only.
Work a further 20 rows st st.
Place a marker at each end of last row.

Overlap and buttonhole band

Work a further 22 rows st st.
Change to 4.5mm needles.
Work 2 rows in moss st.
Buttonhole row: Moss st 7, (work 2tog, yrn, moss st 14) 4 times, work 2tog, yrn, moss st 8.
Work 3 rows in moss st.
Cast off in moss st.

Alternatives

The cushion cover could be just a simple circle with no rosettes, or the rosettes could be placed in different positions. Try pink and lilac for a feminine look, or one colour for a simple design. The flowers can be used on other projects too.

ROSETTES

(make 8)

Using 4.5mm needles and C, cast on 113 sts.
Row 1: K1, (k2, pass 1st st over 2nd st) to end (57 sts).
Row 2: Purl to end.
Row 3: K1, (k2 tog) to end (29 sts).
Row 4: P1, (p2tog) to end (15 sts).
Row 5: As row 3 (8 sts).
Break off yarn, leaving a piece approx 10in (25cm) long. Draw through remaining sts and fasten off tightly, but do not break off yarn (this can be used to attach to cushion cover).

FINISHING OFF

Pin one rosette at centre of circle motif, and secure. Pin the rest of the rosettes closely around the first one, and secure. Using coloured threads to denote fold line, sew side seams. Sew on buttons.

Key to chart

▨	**A** shade 25
☐	**B** shade 01

1 square represents 1 stitch and 1 row

ROSETTE CUSHION COVER CHART
(51 sts x 66 rows)

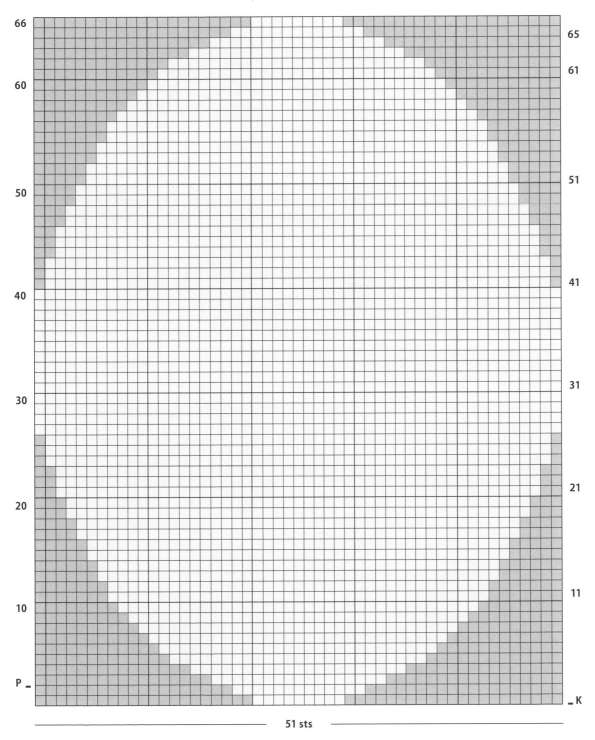

51 sts

Textured
hot water bottle cover

Soft alpaca in a warm neutral with cream is used for this hot water bottle cover.
The simple textured stitch forms a tactile surface topped with fresh stripes for
a hot water bottle that everyone will want to cuddle up to.

YOU WILL NEED
Artesano Alpaca Aran, 50% alpaca, 50% wool
(144yd/132m per 100g hank)
2 hanks Ash (shade C969) (A)
1 hank Strathy (shade SFN10) (B)
A pair of 5.5mm (US9:UK5) needles

FINISHED SIZE
9in (23cm) wide x 13in (33cm) deep

TENSION
18 sts and 24 rows to 4in (10cm) over
pattern using 5.5mm needles.

BACK AND FRONT ALIKE

Using 5.5mm needles and A, cast on 41 sts.
Knit 1 row.
Cont in patt.
Row 1: (RS) K1, p3, (CN1, p3) to last st, k1.
Row 2: K4, (p3, k3) to last st, k1.
Row 3: K1, p3, (k3, p3) to last st, k1.
Row 4: K4, (p3tog, k3) to last st, k1.
Row 5: P to end.
Row 6: K to end.
Row 7: K1, p1, (CN1, p3) to last 3 sts, CN1, p1, k1.
Row 8: K2, (p3, k3) to last 5 sts, p3, k2.
Row 9: K1, p1, (k3, p3) to last 5 sts, k3, p1, k1.
Row 10: K2, (p3tog, k3) to last 5 sts, p3tog, k2.
Row 11: P to end.
Row 12: K to end.
These 12 rows form the patt and are repeated throughout.
Repeat these 12 rows until work measures 27cm, finishing with a wrong-side row.
Eyelet row: K1, (k2tog, yf, k2) to end.
Next row: K to end.
With RS facing, join in B, and k (2 rows B, 2 rows A) twice, k1 row B.
Cast-off row: Using B, cast on 2 sts, (cast off 6 sts, sl remaining st back onto left-hand needle, cast on 2 sts) to last 5 sts, cast off.

FINISHING OFF

Sew up side and bottom seams.

TIE

Cut four 39in (100cm) lengths of A and two lengths of B.
Plait, and knot at each end, leaving a little beyond knot. Thread through eyelets to form a tie.

Alternatives

The cover could also be worked entirely in the garter-stitch stripes used for the top. Try brights or pastels for a different look. The textured stitch would look good on a cushion cover.

Guest bedroom

SOFT TONES OF **LILAC** AND **CREAM** FORM
THE PALETTE FOR THE GUEST BEDROOM. **TEXTURED**
LACE, **PATCHWORK** AND THE SCENT OF **LAVENDER**
COMBINE TO MAKE THIS A **WELCOME** ROOM FOR
YOUR GUESTS, WITH A **NOSTALGIC** FEEL.

Lavender

Flower squares bedcover

Diamond bolster cushion

Flower & check lavender bags

& lace

Flower squares bedcover

Eco wool yarn is used in classic cream for this pretty patchwork bedcover. Tactile bobbles, eyelets and bobble flowers have a comforting nostalgic look to make your guests feel warm and welcome.

YOU WILL NEED

Sirdar Eco DK 100% Undyed Virgin Wool (109yd/100m per 50g ball)
24 balls Ecru 200
1 pair of 4mm (UK8:US6) needles
1 circular 4mm (UK8:US6) needle

FINISHED SIZE

Approx. 53in (134cm) wide x 34in (87cm) long

TENSION

22 sts and 28 rows to 4in (10cm) over st st using 4mm needles.

Alternatives

As this is made in squares, any number can be knitted for different sizes. Try bright colours for a child's room, or neutrals for a throw in a lounge. A cushion cover could be made with four squares.

LARGE FLOWER MOTIF
(make 30)

Leaving a 12in (30cm) end of yarn for sewing up, cast on 31 sts.

Beg with a purl row, work 8 rows in rev st st. Now work flower.

Row 1: (RS) P13, k2, p1, k2, p13.

Row 2: K13, p2, k1, p2, k13.

Row 3: P12, k2tog, k1, yrn, p1, yrn, k1, skpo, p12.

Row 4: K12, p3, k1, p3, k12.

Row 5: P11, k2tog, k1, yrn, k1, p1, k1, yrn, k1, skpo, p11.

Row 6: K11, p4, k1, p4, k11.

Row 7: P10, k2tog, k1, yrn, k2, p1, k2, yrn, k1, skpo, p10.

Row 8: K10, p5, k1, p5, k10.

Row 9: P9, k2tog, k1, yrn, k3, p1, k3, yrn, k1, skpo, p9.

Row 10: K9, p6, k1, p6, k9.

Row 11: P8, (k2tog, k1, yf, k1) twice, yf, k1, skpo, k1, yf, k1, skpo, p8.

Row 12: K8, p6, k1, p1, k1, p6, k8.

Row 13: P8, k3, k2tog, k1, yrn, p1, k1, p1, yrn, k1, skpo, k3, p8.

Row 14: K8, p5, k2, p1, k2, p5, k8.

Row 15: P8, k2, k2tog, k1, yrn, p2, k1, p2, yrn, k1, skpo, k2, p8.

Row 16: K8, p4, k3, p1, k3, p4, k8.

Row 17: P8, k1, k2tog, k1, yrn, p3, k1, p3, yrn, k1, skpo, k1, p8.

Row 18: K8, p3, k4, p1, k4, p3, k8.

Row 19: P8, k2tog, k1, yrn, p3, MB, p1, MB, p3, yrn, k1, skpo, p8.

Row 20: K8, p2, k11, p2, k8.

Row 21: P12, MB, p5, MB, p12.

Row 22: K31.

Row 23: P11, MB, p1, (p2tog, yrn) twice, p2, MB, p11.

Row 24: K31.

Row 25: P11, MB, (p2tog, yrn) 3 times, p1, MB, p11.

Row 26: K31.

Row 27: P11, MB, p1, (p2tog, yrn) twice, p2, MB, p11.

Row 28: K31.

Row 29: P12, MB, p5, MB, p12.

Row 30: K31.

Row 31: P14, MB, p1, MB, p14.

This completes the flower motif.

Beg with a knit row, work 9 rows rev st st.

Cast off, leaving a 12in (30cm) end for sewing up.

SMALL FLOWER MOTIF
(make 30)

Leaving a 12in (30cm) end of yarn for sewing up, cast on 31 sts.

Row 1: (RS) K to end.

Row 2 and every wrong side row: P to end.

Row 3: K5, (yf, skpo, k8) twice, yf, skpo, k4.

Row 5: K3, (k2tog, yf, k1, yf, skpo, k5) twice, k2tog, yf, k1, yf, skpo, k3.

Row 7: K5, (MK, k9) twice, MK, k5.

Rows 9 and 11: K to end.

Row 13: K10, yf, skpo, k8, yf, skpo, k9.

Row 15: K8, k2tog, yf, k1, yf, skpo, k5, k2tog, yf, k1, yf, skpo, k8.

Row 17: K10, MK, k9, MK, k10.

Row 19: K to end.

Row 20: P to end.

Rows 21–28: Rep rows 1 to 20 once, then rows 1 to 8 again.

Cast off, leaving a 12in (30cm) end of yarn for sewing up.

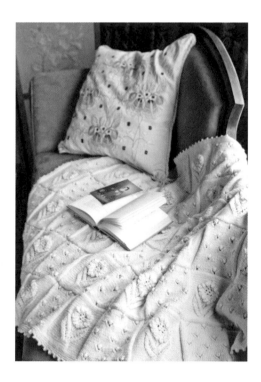

TOP EDGING

Join motifs together to form a rectangle 10 motifs wide by 6 motifs deep.

With right side facing using circular needle, pick up and knit 290 sts along cast-off edges.

Next row: K to end.

Next row: K1, m1, k to last st, m1, k1.

Rep the last 2 rows twice more (296 sts).

Cast-off row: Cast off 4 sts, (cast on 2 sts, cast off 6 sts) to end.

BOTTOM EDGING

With right side facing using circular needle, pick up and knit 290 sts along cast-on edges.

Next row: K to end.

Next row: K1, m1, k to last st, m1, k1.

Rep the last 2 rows twice more (296 sts).

Cast-off row: Cast off 4 sts, (cast on 2 sts, cast off 6 sts) to end.

SIDE EDGINGS
(alike)

With right side facing using circular needle, pick up and knit 178 sts along side edges.

Next row: K to end.

Next row: K1, m1, k to last st, m1, k1.

Rep the last 2 rows twice more (184 sts).

Cast-off row: Cast off 4 sts, (cast on 2 sts, cast off 6 sts) to end.

FINISHING

Join corners.

85

Diamond
bolster cushion

A deeply textured diamond and bobble stitch pattern forms the base for this unusual bolster cushion cover, ideal if you fancy trying a variation on the traditional square cushion shape.

YOU WILL NEED

Debbie Bliss Fez (Aran)
85% wool,15% camel
(39yd/100m per 50g ball)
5 balls shade 10
Pair each of 4mm (US6:UK8) and 4.5mm (US7:UK7) knitting needles
Bolster cushion pad 18in (46cm) long and 8in (20cm) diameter
6 buttons, approx. 1in (2cm) diameter

FINISHED SIZE

Approx. 18in (46cm) long and 8in (20cm) diameter

TENSION

20 sts and 28 rows to 4in (10cm) over pattern using 4.5mm needles.

Alternatives

You can also use this pattern for a more traditional square-shaped cushion by knitting to the correct size and adding a plain back.

CUSHION

With 4mm needles cast on 92 sts.
Knit 8 rows.
Change to 4.5mm needles.

Commence patt

Row 1: (WS) P1, k3, p4, (k6, p4) to last 4 sts, k3, p1.
Row 2: K2, p2, (Cr2R, Cr2L, p2, mb, p2) to last 8 sts, Cr2R, Cr2L, p2, k2.
Row 3: P2, k2, p1, k2, p1, (k2, p2, k2, p1, k2, p1) to last 4 sts, k2, p2.
Row 4: K2, p1, (Cr2Rp, p2, Cr2Lp, p1, k2, p1) to last 9 sts, Cr2Rp, p2, Cr2Lp, p1, k2.
Row 5: P2, k1, p1, k4, (p1, k1, p2, k1, p1, k4) to last 4 sts, p1, k1, p2.
Row 6: K2, (Cr2Rp, p4, Cr2Lp, k2) to last 10 sts, Cr2Rp, p4, Cr2Lp, k2.
Row 7: P3, (k6, p4) to last 9 sts, k6, p3.
Row 8: K1, (Cr2Lp, p2, mb, p2, Cr2Rp) to last st, k1.
Row 9: P1, k1, (p1, k2, p2, k2, p1, k2) to last 10 sts, p1, k2, p2, k2, p1, k1, p1.
Row 10: K1, p1, (Cr2Lp, p1, k2, p1, Cr2Rp, p2) to last 10 sts, Cr2Lp, p1, k2, p1, Cr2Rp, p1, k1.
Row 11: P1, k2, (p1, k1, p2, k1, p1, k4) to last 9 sts, p1, k1, p2, k1, p1, k2, p1.
Row 12: K1, p2, (Cr2Lp, k2, Cr2Rp, p4) to last 9 sts, Cr2Lp, k2, Cr2Rp, p2, k1.
These 12 rows form the patt.
Cont in patt until work measures 24in (60cm) ending with a wrong-side row.
Change to 4mm needles.

Knit 4 rows.
Buttonhole row: K7, k2tog, yf, (k13, k2tog, yf) 5 times, k8.
Knit 4 rows.
Cast off.

END PIECES
(both alike)

Using 4mm needles, cast on 111 sts.
Row 1: K to end.
Row 2: (K9, k2tog) 10 times, k1 (101 sts).
Knit 3 rows.
Row 6: (K8, k2tog) 10 times, k1 (91 sts).
Knit 3 rows.
Row 10: (K7, k2tog) 10 times, k1 (81 sts).
Knit 3 rows.
Row 14: (K6, k2tog) 10 times, k1 (71 sts).
Knit 3 rows.
Row 18: (K5, k2tog) 10 times, k1 (61 sts).
Knit 3 rows.
Row 22: (K4, k2tog) 10 times, k1 (51 sts).
Knit 3 rows.
Row 26: (K3, k2 tog) 10 times, k1 (41 sts).
Knit 3 rows.
Row 30: (K2, k2tog) 10 times, k1 (31 sts).
Knit 3 rows.
Row 34: (K1, k2tog) 10 times, k1 (21 sts).
Knit 3 rows.
Row 38: (K2 tog) 10 times, k1 (11 sts).
Knit 1 row.
Row 40: (K2tog) 5 times, k1 (6 sts).
Leaving a long end, cut off yarn and thread through rem 6 sts, draw up tight and fasten off. Join seam.

FINISHING

Place buttonhole band over button band and catch row ends in place. Sew on buttons. Sew end pieces to row ends of main piece. Make two tassels and then sew one to the centre of each end.

Flower & check lavender bags

The bamboo- and viscose-mix yarn used for these lavender bags is beautifully soft and silky. A flower motif taken from the bedcover on page 82 and traditional checks are tied with ribbon for a nostalgic look and filled with dried lavender.

YOU WILL NEED
Sublime Bamboo and Pearls DK,
70% bamboo viscose, 30% pearl viscose
(104yd/95m per 50g ball)
For the flower bag:
1 ball Neroli (shade 208)
For the checked bag:
1 ball each of:
Oyster (shade 215) (A)
Neroli (shade 208) (B)
For both bags:
A pair of size 4mm (US6:UK8) needles
Dried lavender flowers
Piece of thin fabric 13 x 6in (33 x 15cm)

20in (50cm) length of narrow ribbon
(approx. $1/2$in/1cm in width)
14in (36cm) length of wider ribbon
(approx. $1^1/_4$in/2.5cm diameter)

FINISHED SIZE
Both bags are $5^1/_2$in (14cm) wide by
7in (18cm) high

TENSION
22 sts and 28 rows to 4in (10cm) over st st
using 4mm needles.

Alternatives

Any stitch or pattern can be used to make
these simple bags. Use different dried
flowers for each room to vary the scents.

FLOWER LAVENDER BAG
Front

Using 4mm needles cast on 31 sts.
Beg with a purl row, work 8 rows in rev st st.
Now work flower motif.
Row 1: (RS) P13, k2, p1, k2, p13.
Row 2: K13, p2, k1, p2, k13.
Row 3: P12, k2tog, k1, yrn, p1, yrn, k1, skpo, p12.
Row 4: K12, p3, k1, p3, k12.
Row 5: P11, k2tog, k1, yrn, k1, p1, k1, yrn, k1,
skpo, p11.
Row 6: K11, p4, k1, p4, k11.
Row 7: P10, k2tog, k1, yrn, k2, p1, k2, yrn, k1,
skpo, p10.
Row 8: K10, p5, k1, p5, k10.
Row 9: P9, k2tog, k1, yrn, k3, p1, k3, yrn, k1,
skpo, p9.
Row 10: K9, p6, k1, p6, k9.
Row 11: P8, (k2tog, k1, yf, k1) twice, yf, k1, skpo,
k1, yf, k1, skpo, p8.

Row 12: K8, p6, k1, p1, k1, p6, k8.
Row 13: P8, k3, k2tog, k1, yrn, p1, k1, p1, yrn, k1,
skpo, k3, p8.
Row 14: K8, p5, k2, p1, k2, p5, k8.
Row 15: P8, k2, k2tog, k1, yrn, p2, k1, p2, yrn, k1,
skpo, k2, p8.
Row 16: K8, p4, k3, p1, k3, p4, k8.
Row 17: P8, k1, k2tog, k1, yrn, p3, k1, p3, yrn, k1,
skpo, k1, p8.
Row 18: K8, p3, k4, p1, k4, p3, k8.
Row 19: P8, k2tog, k1, yrn, p3, MB, p1, MB, p3,
yrn, k1, skpo, p8.
Row 20: K8, p2, k11, p2, k8.
Row 21: P12, MB, p5, MB, p12.
Row 22: K31.
Row 23: P11, MB, p1, (p2tog, yrn) twice, p2,
MB, p11.
Row 24: K31.
Row 25: P11, MB, (p2tog, yrn) 3 times, p1,
MB, p11.
Row 26: K31.
Row 27: P11, MB, p1, (p2tog, yrn) twice, p2,
MB, p11.
Row 28: K31.
Row 29: P12, MB, p5, MB, p12.
Row 30: K31.
Row 31: P14, MB, p1, MB, p14.
This completes the flower motif.

Beginning with a knit row, work 8 rows rev st st.
** Eyelet row: K2, k2tog, yf, (k6, k2tog, yf) to last 3 sts, k3.
Knit 4 rows.
Next row: K1, skpo, knit to last 3 sts, k2tog, k1 (29 sts).
Picot cast-off row: Cast off 2 sts, (slip remaining st on right-hand needle back onto left-hand needle, cast on 2 sts, cast off 4 sts) to end and fasten off remaining st **.

Back

Cast on 31 sts.
Beginning with a purl row, work 47 rows rev st st. Work as for front from ** to **.

Finishing flower bag

Join side seams. Fold over fabric, turn over edges and sew two sides on a sewing machine. Fill with lavender flowers. Sew up remaining side. Place inside knitted bag. Thread narrow ribbon through eyelets. Sew wider ribbon to top to form a handle.

CHECK LAVENDER BAG
Back and Front (alike)

Using 4mm needles and B, cast on 38 sts.
Row 1: K2B, (2A, 2B) to end.
Row 2: P2B, (2A, 2B) to end.
Row 3: K2A, (2B, 2A) to end.
Row 4: P2A, (2B, 2A) to end.
These 4 rows form the pattern.
Work a further 42 rows.
Eyelet row: Using A, k4, k2tog, yf, (k5, k2tog, yf) to last 4 sts, k4.
Using A, knit 3 rows.
Cut off A.
Using B, knit 1 row.
Picot cast-off row: Cast off 2 sts, (slip remaining st on right-hand needle back onto left-hand needle, cast on 2 sts, cast off 4 sts) to end and fasten off remaining 2 sts.

Finishing checked bag

Press pieces according to yarn band instructions. Sew pieces together. Sew sides of fabric on sewing machine. Put lavender flowers inside. Sew remaining seam. Place inside knitted bag. Thread narrow ribbon through eyelets. Attach wider ribbon to top to form handle.

Secret garden bedroom

BUTTERFLIES AND **FLOWERS** ARE THE THEME FOR THIS BEDROOM. INSPIRED BY A **COUNTRY GARDEN** IN GLORIOUS SUMMER, **PRETTY** THREE-DIMENSIONAL MOTIFS HELP TO CREATE A **MAGICAL** ROOM.

Butterflies

Butterfly & flower curtain

Butterfly cushion cover

Hearts & flowers toy bag

& flowers

Butterfly & flower curtain

Mercerized cotton in a colourful palette is used for this delightful curtain. Butterflies and flowers are attached to long i-cords, to decorate a window or to make a dramatic entrance to this country garden-inspired room.

YOU WILL NEED
Patons 100% Cotton DK
(230yd/210m per 100g ball)
3 balls Cream (shade 692) (A)
1 ball each of:
Nougat (shade 715) (B)
Candy (shade 734) (C)
Cheeky (shade 719) (D)
Sky (shade 702) (E)
Lilac (shade 701) (F)
Neroli (shade 741) (G)
Note: this amount is for 8 i-cords, a mix of flowers and butterflies totalling 51 flowers and 57 butterflies. Make more or fewer as required.
A pair of 2.75mm (US2:UK12) needles
2 x 2.75mm (US2:UK12) double-pointed needles

Piece of dowelling, to fit the width of the doorway or window (this one is $^1/_2$in/12mm diameter, $31^1/_2$in/80cm wide)
Cup hooks to secure dowelling

FINISHED SIZE
This is made to fit the width and length of your window or doorway. Instructions are given for an opening 31in (80cm) wide and 80in (204cm) high.

TENSION
Tension is not critical for this project.

Alternatives

The flowers and butterflies could be used on many different projects. Try using them to brighten up a simple cushion cover or throw, on bags, or used around the room as decorations.

FLOWERS
(make 17 in each colourway)

Colourway 1: F, B, A.
Colourway 2: B, C, A.
Colourway 3: C, F, A.
Using 2.75mm needles and A, cast on one st, k into front, back and front of st (3 sts).
Row 1: P to end.
Row 2: K1, m1, k1, m1, k1 (5sts).
Row 3: P to end.
Row 4: K to end.
Row 5: P to end.
Row 6: Skpo, k1, k2tog (3 sts).
Row 7: Sl1, p2tog, psso.
Fasten off, leaving a length of yarn.
With RS facing, make a running st around outer edge and pull tight to form a ball. Secure, leaving a loose end. These will be used to sew into centre of flower.

Top petals
(make 5 per flower, worked in garter st)

Using 2.75mm needles and F (B, C), cast on 3 sts.
Row 1: K1, m1, k1, m1, k1 (5 sts).
Row 2: Knit to end.
Row 3: K1, m1, k3, m1, k1 (7 sts).
Row 4: As row 2.
Fasten off. Leave sts on the needle being used. Starting with this needle, make 3 more petals, leaving them on the same needle, then make

one more petal (5 in total). Do not fasten off.
Next row: K2, sl1, k2tog, psso, k2 across last petal worked. Rep across the following 4 petals so that there are 5 petals on one needle (25 sts).
Next row: K1, (k2tog) to end (13 sts).
Rep last row once more (7 sts).
Leave a small length of yarn. Using a tapestry needle, thread through remaining sts, pull tight and fasten off.

Outer petals
(worked as one piece)

Using 2.75mm needles and B (C, F), cast on 9 sts.
Row 1: P to end.
Row 2: K to end.
Row 3: Cast off 6 sts purlwise, p to end.
* Row 4: K to end.
Row 5: Cast on 6 sts, p to end.
Row 6: K to end.
Row 7: As row 3 *.
Rep from * to * 3 times more.
Next row: K to end.
Cast off knitwise, leaving a length of yarn with RS facing. Join cast-off and cast-on edges together to form a circle.
Turn petals over to WS facing, thread length of yarn around inner centre edge, pull together and secure.

Finishing flowers

Sew bobble to centre of top petals, place lower petals underneath top petals, arranging it so that the lower petals can be seen. Sew in place. Press petals carefully.

BUTTERFLIES
(make 19 in each colourway)

Colourway 1: G, E, A.
Colourway 2: D, E, A.
Colourway 3: E, D, A.

Top wings
(make two per butterfly)
Worked in garter st and short rows.
Using 2.75mm needles and G (D, E),
cast on 7 sts.
Rows 1 and 2: K to end.
Rows 3 and 4: K2, turn, k to end.
Rows 5 and 6: K4, turn, k to end.
Rows 7 and 8: K6, turn, k to end.
Rows 9 and 10: K4, turn, k to end.
Rows 11 and 12: K2, turn, k to end.
Rows 13 and 14: K to end.
Cast off knitwise.

Wing edging
Using 2.75mm needles and E (E, D), with
RS of wing facing, pick up 9 sts along widest
part of the wing edge (outer edge), turn.
Next row: Cast off knitwise.
Repeat for 2nd wing.

Lower wings
Worked in one piece.
Using 2.75mm needles and G (D, E), cast on 16 sts.
Rows 1 and 2: K to end.
Row 3: K2, skpo, k to last 4 sts, 2tog, k2.
Row 4: K to end.
Rows 5–10: Rep rows 3 and 4 three times (8 sts).
Row 11: K to end.
Cast off knitwise, leaving a length of yarn. With
this and a tapestry needle, make a running
st through the centre of the lower wing, pull
together to slightly gather the centre of the
wings, secure in place.

Body
Using 2.75mm double-pointed needles and A,
cast on 3 sts.
Row 1: K to end, do not turn work.
Row 2: Slip sts to the other end of the needle,
take yarn across back of work, pull tightly, k3,
do not turn work.

Rep row 2 until i-cord measures 1³/₄ins (4.5cm)
Next row: Sl1, k2tog, psso.
Fasten off.

Finishing butterflies
Sew top wings together. Slightly overlap top
wings to lower wings, sew in place. Work a
French knot in E (E, D) onto left and right lower
corners of bottom wings. Sew body onto centre
of wings. Using a single thread of A, make an
antenna, secure, and knot each end, cut to
neaten ends.
Press wings carefully.

I-CORDS
(make 8)
Using 2.75mm double-pointed needles and A,
cast on 4 sts.
Row 1: Knit to end, do not turn work.
Row 2: Slip sts to the other end of the needle,
take yarn across back of work, pull tightly, k4,
do not turn work.
Rep row 2 until the i-cord measures the correct
length for your door frame.

COVER FOR TOP POLE
(make to fit width of doorway or window)
Using 2.75mm double-pointed needles and A,
cast on 15 sts.
Beg with a knit row work in st st until work
measures 31¹/₂ins (80cm).
Leaving a long end, cut off yarn and thread
through sts.
Fasten tightly, using the yarn to sew the row
ends together.
Sew long seam.
Once pole has been put in, sew end with
a gathering thread.

FINISHING OFF
Attach butterflies and flowers to i-cords.
Attach i-cords to top pole.

Butterfly cushion cover

Merino Aran in colourful brights gives this pretty cushion cover a cozy feel. A striking butterfly motif is surrounded by tactile three-dimensional flowers, making a fun project for a garden-themed child's bedroom.

YOU WILL NEED

Rico Soft Merino Aran, 100% wool
(109yd/100m per 50g ball)
4 balls Light Blue (shade 033) (A)
2 balls each of:
Fuchsia (shade 015) (B)
Eucalyptus (shade 041) (C)
1 ball Pistachio (shade 050) (D)
A pair each of 4.5mm (US7:UK7) and 5mm
(US8:UK6) needles
6 buttons, approx. 1¼in (2.5cm) diameter
Cushion pad 18 x 18in (45 x 45cm)

FINISHED SIZE

18 x 18in (45 x 45cm)

TENSION

18 sts and 24 rows to 4in (10cm) over st st using 5mm needles.

PATTERN NOTES

When working from chart, right-side rows are knit rows and read from right to left. Wrong-side rows are purl rows and read from left to right. Use separate balls of yarn for each area of colour and twist yarn on wrong side to avoid a hole when changing colour.

BUTTERFLY CUSHION COVER CHART
(54 sts x 72 rows)

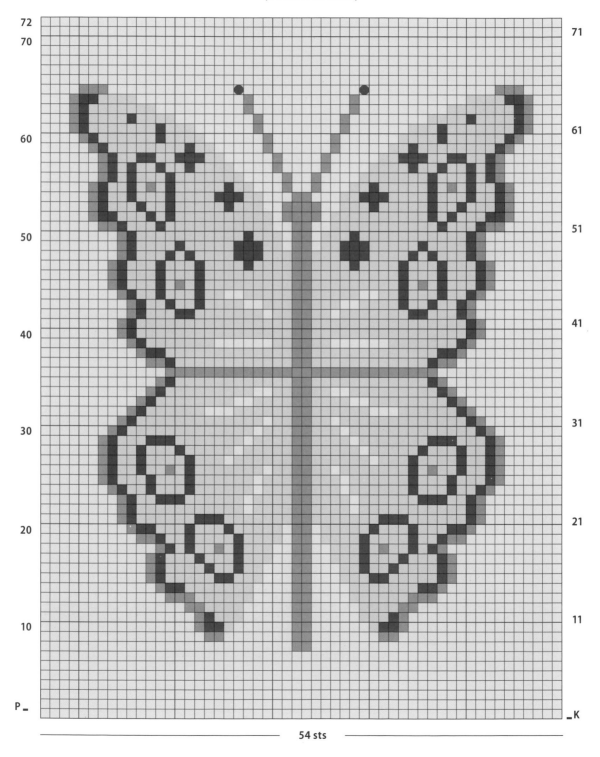

54 sts

CUSHION COVER

Knitted in one piece starting at top back.

Using 4.5mm needles and A, cast on 86 sts.

Button border

Moss st row 1: (K1, p1) to end.

Moss st row 2: (P1, k1) to end.

These 2 rows form the moss st.

Work a further 4 rows.

Change to 5mm needles.

Beg with a knit row, work 92 rows in st st.

Place a marker at each end of last row.

Front

Work a further 8 rows st st.

Working in the intarsia method, work as follows:

Next row: K7A, 72D, 7A.

Next row: P7A, 72D, 7A.

Rep these 2 rows 5 more times.

Now work from chart.

Rows 1, 3, 5 and 7: K7A, 9D, 54A, 9D, 7A.

Rows 2, 4 and 6: P7A, 9D, 54A, 9D, 7A.

Row 8: P7A, 9D, work across 54 sts of row 8 of chart, k9D, 7A.

Row 9: K7A, 9D, work across 54 sts of row 9 of chart, k9D, 7A.

Rows 8 and 9 set the chart and form the border in D and A.

Continue as set until all 72 rows of chart have been worked.

Next row: K7A, 72D, 7A.

Next row: P7A, 72D, 7A.

Rep these 2 rows 5 more times.

Continue in A only.

Work a further 8 rows st st.

Place a marker at each end of last row.

Overlap and buttonhole band

Work a further 16 rows st st.

Change to 4.5mm needles.

Work 2 rows in moss st.

Buttonhole row: Moss st 12, (work 2tog, yrn, moss st 10) 5 times, work 2tog, yrn, moss st 12.

Work 3 rows in moss st.

Cast off in moss st.

ROSETTES

(make 8 in B and 8 in C).

Using 4.5mm needles cast on 113 sts.

Row 1: K1, (k2, pass 1st st over 2nd st) to end (57 sts).

Row 2: P to end.

Row 3: K1, (k2tog) to end (29 sts).

Row 4: P1, (p2tog) to end (15 sts).

Row 5: As row 3 (8 sts).

Break off yarn, leaving a length approx 10in (25cm) long. Draw through remaining sts and fasten off tightly, but do not break off yarn (this can be used to attach to cushion cover).

FINISHING OFF

Press according to yarn band instructions. Place rosettes on the border, alternating the colours, sew in place. Using B, work a large French knot at end of each antenna. Fold cushion cover to correspond to markers, overlap top back button band border. Sew in place. Sew on buttons to correspond with buttonholes.

Key to chart

☐	**A** Light Blue	☐	K on RS, P on WS
■	**B** Fuchsia	◉	K on WS, P on RS
▦	**C** Eucalyptus		
☐	**D** Pistachio		

1 square represents 1 stitch and 1 row

Hearts & flowers toy bag

Colourful cotton Aran is used for this attractive toy bag. Simple flower and moss-stitch heart intarsia motifs are surrounded by embroidered flowers and French knots for a sweet and practical project.

YOU WILL NEED
Debbie Bliss Eco Aran Fairtrade Collection, 100% cotton (82yd/75m per 50g ball)
5 balls shade 610 (A)
1 ball each of:
shade 612 (B)
shade 619 (C)
Oddments of shade 609 (D) for embroidery
A pair each of 4mm (US6:UK8) and 4.5mm (US7:UK7) needles
117in (3m) silky rope for handle

FINISHED SIZE
17in (44cm) deep x 14in (35cm) wide

TENSION
18 sts and 24 rows to 4in (10cm) over st st using 4.5mm needles.

PATTERN NOTES
When working from chart, right-side rows are knit rows and read from right to left. Wrong-side rows are purl rows and read from left to right. Use separate balls of yarn for each area of colour and twist yarn on wrong side to avoid a hole when changing colour.

TOY BAG

Using 4mm needles and A, cast on 65 sts.

Moss st row: K1, (p1, k1) to end.

This row forms the moss st border.

Work a further 8 rows.

Change to 4.5mm needles.

Eyelet row: (WS) P4, (p2tog, yrn, p9) 5 times, p2tog, yrn, p4.

Beg with a knit row, work 100 rows in st st.

Place a marker at each end of the last row.

Work a further 6 rows.

Place heart motif as follows.

Row 1: K21A, patt across 23 sts of row 1 of chart, k21A.

Row 2: P21A, patt across 23 sts of row 2 of chart, p21A.

Continue working in st st following chart until 25 rows have been completed.

Using A, work a further 3 rows in st st.

Place flower motif as follows.

Row 1: K21A, patt across 23 sts of row 1 of chart, k21A.

Row 2: P21A, patt across 23 sts of row 2 of chart, p21A.

Continue working in st st following chart until 31 rows of chart have been completed.

Using A, work a further 3 rows in st st.

Place heart motif as follows.

Row 1: K21A, patt across 23 sts of row 1 of chart, k21A.

Row 2: P21A, patt across 23 sts of row 2 of chart, p21A.

Continue working in st st following chart until 25 rows have been completed.

Work 6 rows in A in st st.

Eyelet row: (WS) P4, (p2tog, yrn, p9) 5 times, p2tog, yrn, p4.

Change to 4mm needles.

Work 9 rows in moss st.

Cast off in moss st.

FINISHING OFF

Embroider French knots at centre of flower motif and around petals using yarn D. Embroider scattered flowers around background. Join side seams. Cut six pieces of yarn 59in (150cm) long. Make a plait and thread through eyelets to form a tie. Cut 3 x 39in (1m) lengths of rope, and form a plait. Sew at inside top to form a handle.

Alternatives

The motifs can be used on other projects. Try them on a cushion cover with the embroidered motifs around them, or knit in squares to form a bedcover.

Heart chart

(23 sts x 25 rows)

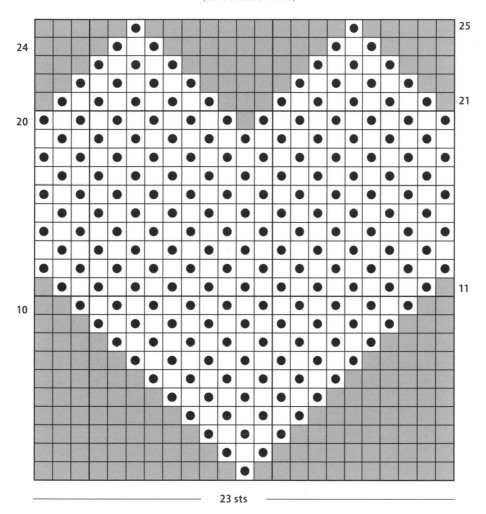

23 sts

Key to chart

▦	**A** shade 610	☐	K on RS, P on WS
☐	**C** shade 619	⦿	K on WS, P on RS

1 square represents 1 stitch and 1 row

Flower chart

(23 sts x 31 rows)

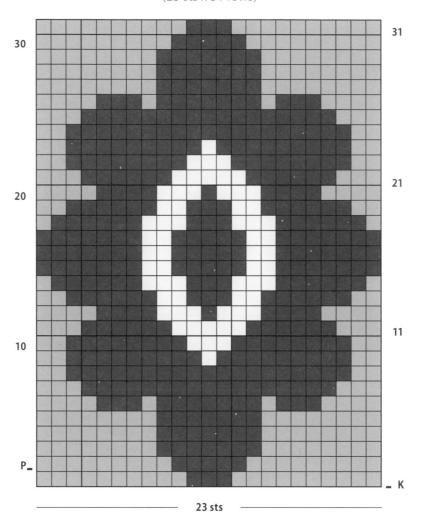

23 sts

Key to chart

A shade 610
B shade 612
C shade 619

1 square represents 1 stitch and 1 row

Pirate's bedroom

LAND AHOY FOR AN EXCITING **DEEP SEA ADVENTURE**. **PIRATES**, **ANCHORS** AND **SEAWEED** COME TOGETHER TO CREATE A **MAGICAL MARINE** WORLD THAT KIDS WILL LOVE.

All at sea

Seaweed door curtain

Anchor floor cushion

Jolly Roger toy bag

Seaweed
door curtain

Mercerized cotton in blues and greens is used for this imaginative crochet project. The pods and twirls of seaweed inspire the stitches to make a fun entrance to the deep-sea-themed room.

YOU WILL NEED

Patons 100% Cotton DK
(230yd/210m per 100g ball)
3 balls each of:
Moss (shade 731) (A)
Orchard (shade 721) (B)
Denim (shade 697) (C)
2.5mm (USC/2:UK12) and 3mm (USD/3:UK10) crochet hooks
Piece of dowelling to fit the width of doorway (this one is 1/2in (12mm) diameter, 31 1/2in (80cm) wide
Cup hooks to secure dowelling

FINISHED SIZE

Instructions are given for a door 31in (80cm) wide and 80in (204cm) high.

TENSION

Tension is not critical for this project.

PATTERN NOTES

This curtain is constructed using separate strings of twists and pods with cords between. They can be worked randomly, placing pods and twists and colour changes where you want them. You can make as many strings as you like. This one has 15 in total – 11 twirls and 4 pods.

CORDS AND PODS
(make 1 in A, 2 in B and 1 in C)

To achieve an individual look, work the cord and pods with varying distances between them.

Foundation ring

Using 2.5mm hook, make loop by wrapping yarn around forefinger, take off finger, still holding between thumb and forefinger, insert hook through loop, yrh (1 loop on hook), draw through loop, yrh, draw through loop (making a sl st to hold loop together). Work 6dc into circle, pull loose end to close the circle, weave end into the WS of work on 2nd round, sl st into 1st dc of round. Do not turn, keep working in rounds.

** Round 1: 3ch (counts as 1st tr), miss 1st dc, 1tr into each dc, sl st into top of 3ch at beg of round (6 tr).

Round 2: 3ch (counts as 1st tr), 1tr into each of remaining 5tr, sl st into top of 3ch (6 tr). Repeat round 2 four times more.

Place pod

Round 1: 1ch, 1dc into each tr including 3ch at beg of round, sl st into top of dc at beg of round (6 dc).

Round 2: 1ch, 1dc into same place as 1ch, 2dc into next dc, 1dc into each of next 2dc, 2dc into next dc, 1dc into last dc, sl st into 1st dc (8 dc).

Round 3: 1ch, 2dc into each dc (16 dc). Sl st into 1st dc.

Rounds 4–7: 1ch, 1dc into each dc, sl st into 1st dc (16 dc).

Round 8: 1ch, (dc2tog) 8 times, sl st into 1st dc (8dc).

Round 9: 1ch, 1dc into 1st dc, dc2tog over next 2dc, 1dc into each of next 2dc, dc2tog over next 2dc, 1dc into last dc, sl st into 1st dc (6 dc).

Round 10: 1ch, 1dc into each dc, sl st into 1st dc. Continue working round 1, then only round 2 of treble cords.

Work one more round in trs, place pod again. Repeat the tr cord as before for 9 rows, place pod. **

Repeat from ** to ** until you have reached the correct length for your door frame.

To finish off cord, work the following:

Round 1: 1ch, 1dc into same place as ch, 1dc into each tr, fasten off, leaving a length of yarn, thread and weave around dcs, pull tight, and secure.

TWIRLS
(make 4 in A, 3 in B and 4 in C)

To give the twirls an individual look, shorten or lengthen the distances between them.

Using 3mm hook, make a ch length (the length of your door frame plus an extra quarter of the length). This is to allow shrinkage when working the twirls. Extra chs can be cut off the end.

Row 1: 1dc into 2nd ch from hook, 1dc into each of following ch until the desired length has been reached, allow extra quarter of total length again in length of dc.

Row 2: 3ch, 1tr into 1st dc, 1tr into each of next 4dc, * (3tr into each of next 9dc) twirl made, 1tr into each of next 7dc, (3tr into each of next 15dc) twirl made, 1 tr into each of next 9dc, (3tr into each of next 12 dc) twirl made, 1tr into each of next 5dc; repeat from * to end.

Fasten off.

Note: twist the twirls as you go along for a spiral effect.

To make the twirls as you want them, shorten or lengthen the distance between each group of twirls.

TOP POLE

Using 2.5mm hook, work as for tr cord only. This one is worked as a plain tr i-cord of 9tr. Slide pole into the cord and sew up. (If pole is thicker, add trs to make it fit.)

FINISHING OFF

Sew in ends of cords and twirls to pole in the sequence you prefer.

Alternatives

The pods and twirls can be used in other rooms with colour changes – try blues for a bathroom. Or use as a wall hanging by varying the lengths of the cords and twirls.

Anchor floor cushion

Aran wool is used for this fabulous floor cushion. The large-scale simple anchor motif is striking in classic nautical navy and cream, creating a place to relax and read salty sea tales in this pirate-themed room.

YOU WILL NEED

Garnstudio Alaska, 100% wool
(82yd/75m per 50g ball)
11 balls Navy Blue (shade 12) (A)
1 ball Off White (shade 02) (B)
Cushion pad size 25$\frac{1}{2}$ x 25$\frac{1}{2}$in (65 x 65cm)
7 buttons
A pair of 5mm (US8:UK6) needles

FINISHED SIZE

25$\frac{1}{2}$ x 25$\frac{1}{2}$in (65 x 65cm)

TENSION

17 st and 22 rows to 4in (10cm) over st st using 5mm needles.

PATTERN NOTES

When working from chart, right-side rows are knit rows and read from right to left. Wrong-side rows are purl rows and read from left to right. Use separate balls of yarn for each area of colour and twist yarn on wrong side to avoid a hole when changing colour.

CUSHION

Knitted in one piece starting at top back.

Back

Using 5mm needles and A, cast on 110 sts.
Moss st row 1: (K1, p1) to end.
Moss st row 2: (P1, k1) to end.
These 2 rows form the moss st pattern.
Work 1 more row.
Beg with a knit row, work 130 rows in st st.
Mark each end of last row with a coloured
thread.

Front

Work a further 18 rows st st.
Work in patt from chart.
Row 1: K16A, patt across 79 sts of row 1 of chart,
k15A.
Row 2: P15A, patt across 79 sts of row 2 of chart,
p16A.
These 2 rows set the position of the chart.
Keeping sts in A at each side, continue to follow
chart until 108 rows have been worked.
Continue in A only.
Work a further 18 rows st st.
Place a marker at each end of last row.

Overlap and buttonhole band

Using A, work 10 rows in st st.
Work 2 rows in moss st.
Buttonhole row: Moss st 6, (work 2tog, yrn,
moss st 14) 6 times, work 2tog, yrn, moss st 6.
Work 2 rows in moss st.
Cast off in moss st.

FINISHING OFF

Using coloured threads to denote fold line,
join side seams. Sew on buttons.

Alternatives

Make this into a bedcover or throw by
adding more stitches and rows to the
background, and working a cream edging.

Key to chart
A Navy Blue
☐ **B** Off White
1 square represents 1 stitch and 1 row

ANCHOR FLOOR CUSHION CHART
(79 sts x 108 rows)

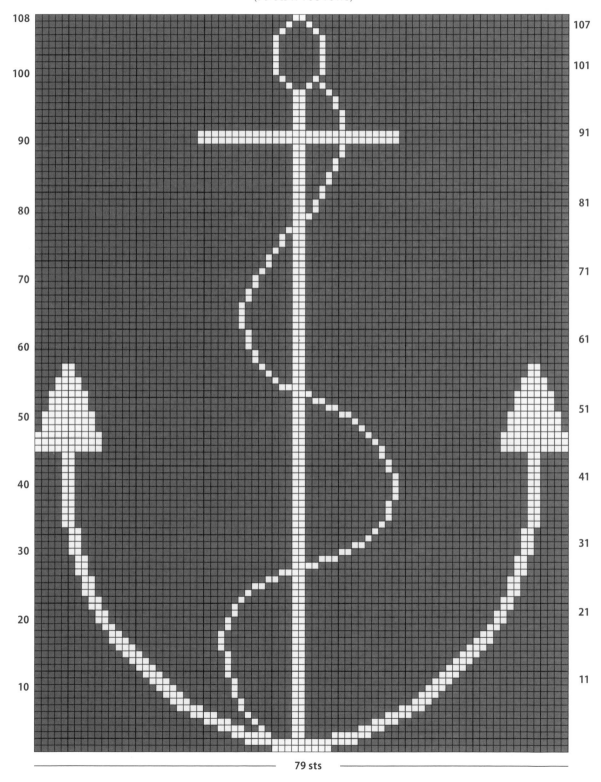

79 sts

Jolly Roger toy bag

The Jolly Roger motif on this quirky toy bag warns that pirates are close by! Cotton Aran is used in strong colours and the bag even has a 'rope' handle for an extra nautical look, making a fun and practical project.

YOU WILL NEED
Debbie Bliss Eco Aran Fairtrade Collection, 100% cotton (82yd/75m per 50g ball)
5 balls shade 616 (A)
1 ball in each of:
shade 608 (B)
shade 613 (C)
shade 618 (D)
A pair each of 4mm (US6:UK8) and 4.5mm (US7:UK7) needles
117in (3m) rope for handle

FINISHED SIZE
17in (44cm) deep x 14in (35cm) wide

TENSION
18 sts and 24 rows to 4in (10cm) over st st using 4.5mm needles.

PATTERN NOTES
When working from chart, right-side rows are knit rows and read from right to left. Wrong-side rows are purl rows and read from left to right. Use separate balls of yarn for each area of colour and twist yarn on wrong side to avoid a hole when changing colour.

JOLLY ROGER TOY BAG CHART
(44 sts x 60 rows)

44 sts

TOY BAG

Knitted in one piece starting at top back.

Using 4mm needles and A, cast on 65 sts.

Knit 11 rows.

Change to 4.5mm needles.

Eyelet row: (WS) P4, (p2tog, yrn, p9) 5 times,
p2tog, yrn, p4.

Beg with a knit row work 100 rows in st st.

Place a marker at each end of the last row.

Work a further 20 rows.

Work in patt from chart.

Row 1: K11A, patt across 44 sts of row 1
of chart, k10A.

Row 2: P10A, patt across 44 sts of row 2
of chart, p11A.

Continue working in st st following chart,
until 60 rows of chart have been completed.

Work 19 rows in A in st st.

Eyelet row: (WS) P4, (p2tog, yrn, p9) 5 times,
p2tog, yrn, p4.

Change to 4mm needles.

Knit 11 rows.

Cast off.

FINISHING

Join side seams, noting that coloured threads
form fold line. Cut six pieces of yarn 59in
(150cm) long. Make a plait and thread through
eyelets to form a tie. Cut 3 x 39in (1m) lengths
of rope, and form a plait. Sew at inside top to
form a handle.

Key to chart

☐	**A**	shade 616
☐	**B**	shade 608
■	**C**	shade 613
■	**D**	shade 618

1 square represents 1 stitch and 1 row

Alternatives

Use the Jolly Roger motif to make a
cushion cover, a throw or a fun wall
hanging on a flagpole.

Nursery

TRADITIONAL **NURSERY RHYMES** HAVE INSPIRED THESE **PLAYFUL** ROOM ACCESSORIES. USING BEAUTIFULLY **SOFT** YARNS, YOUR **LITTLE ONES** WILL LOVE THE **INTERACTIVE** TWIST ON THESE **PRACTICAL** ITEMS.

Humpty Dumpty toy tidy

Hickory Dickory Dock nappy holder

Three little pigs mobile

rhymes

Humpty Dumpty toy tidy

Soft merino cashmere silk is used for this toy tidy, which could be tied to the side of a cot. Humpty sits on the wall and can be taken off to play with, making a unique storage project for small toys.

YOU WILL NEED
Sublime Cashmere Merino Silk DK,
75% wool, 20% silk and 5% cashmere
(127yd/116m per 50g)
3 balls Vanilla (shade 03) (A)
2 balls Very Cherry (shade 164) (B)
1 ball each of Duck (shade 109) (C), Shortbread
(shade 128) (D) and Egg Nog (shade 106) (E)
A pair each of 3.75mm (US5:UK9) and 5mm
(US8:UK6) needles
Two double-pointed 3.75mm (US5:UK9) needles
Toy stuffing
Small pieces of hook-and-loop fastener

FINISHED SIZE
10in (25cm) wide x 12in (30cm) high

TENSION
18 sts and 24 rows to 4in (10cm) over
pattern using 5mm needles and yarn double.

Alternatives

Knit the storage container in one colour
for another room. Humpty can also be used
as a toy on his own.

TOY TIDY

Using 5mm needles and B double, cast on
47 sts.

Knit 3 rows.

Join in A, using yarn doubled.

Work in patt.

Rows 1 and 2: Using A, k to end.

Row 3: K5B, (1A, 3B) to last 2 sts, 2B.

Row 4: K1, p4B, (k1A, p3B) to last 2 sts, k1A, k1B.

Rows 5 and 6: Using A, k to end.

Row 7: (K3B, 1A) to last 3 sts, 3B.

Row 8: K1, p2B, (k1A, p3B) to last 4 sts, k1A,
p2, k1B.

These 8 rows form the patt and are
repeated throughout.

Rep these 8 rows until work measures
23in (59cm), ending with row 2 or 6.

Using B, knit 4 rows.

Cast off.

HUMPTY DUMPTY
Body

Using 3.75mm needles and D, cast on 5 sts.
Purl 1 row.

Next row: Inc in each of next 2 sts, k1, inc in
each of next 2 sts (9 sts).

Next and every following alternate row:
P to end.

Row 1: (K1, m1) to last st, k1 (17 sts).

Row 3: (K2, m1) to last st, k1 (25 sts).

Row 5: (K3, m1) to last st, k1 (33 sts).

Row 7: (K4, m1) to last st, k1 (41 sts).

Row 9: K to end.

Row 11: (K5, m1) to last st, k1 (49 sts).

Row 13: K to end.

Row 15: (K6, m1) to last st, k1 (57 sts).

Break off D, and join in B.

Beginning with a p row, work 3 rows st st.

Break off B.

Join in C.

Row 1: K1, (k2tog, k5) to end (49 sts).

Row 2 and every foll alternate row: P to end.

Row 3: K1, (k2tog, k4) to end (41 sts).

Row 5: K to end.

Row 7: K1, (k2tog, k3) to end (33 sts).

Row 9: K to end.

Row 11: K1, (k2tog, k2) to end (25 sts).

Row 13: K to end.

Row 15: K1, (k2tog, k1) to end (17 sts).

Row 17: K1, (k2tog) to end (9 sts).

Row 18: (P2tog) twice, p1, (p2tog) twice (5 sts).

Break off yarn and thread through
remaining sts.

Pull tight and secure, leaving enough yarn to
sew seam.

Arms
(make 2)

Using 3.75mm double-pointed needles and D,
cast on 5 sts.

Row 1: K to end, do not turn work.

Row 2: Slip sts to the other end of the needle,
take yarn across back of work, pull tightly, k5,
do not turn work.

Rep row 2 until i-cord is 2¹/₂ins (6.5cm) long.
Now work backwards and forwards in rows.

Next row: Knit.

Hands

Row 1: Inc into every st (10 sts).

Row 2 and every alternate row: P to end.

Row 3: (Inc in next st, k1) to end (15 sts).

Row 5: (K1, k2 tog) to end (10 sts).

Row 7: (K2tog) to end (5 sts).

Break off yarn and thread through remaining
sts, pull tight and secure. Join row ends, stuffing
hand lightly.

Legs
(make 2)

With 3.75mm double-pointed needles and D, cast on 5 sts.

Work i-cord as for arms for 3In (8cm).

Break off D.

Join in E.

Now work backwards and forwards in rows.

Next row: Knit.

Feet

Row 1: Inc into every st (10 sts).

Row 2 and every alternate row: P to end.

Row 3: K to end.

Row 5: (Inc in next st, k1) to end (15 sts).

Rows 7 and 9: K to end.

Row 11: (K1, k2tog) to end (10 sts).

Row 13: (K2tog) to end (5 sts).

Break off yarn and thread through remaining sts, pull tight to secure.

Finish as for hands.

Hat

Using 3.75mm needles and B, cast on 44 sts.

Knit 1 row.

Next row: (K2, k2tog) to end (33 sts).

Purl 1 row.

Next row: (K1, k2tog) to end (22 sts).

Purl 3 rows.

Starting with a knit row, work 7 rows st st.

Knit 1 row.

Next row: K1, (k2tog, k1) to end (15 sts).

Next and following alternate row: P to end.

Next row: K1, (k2tog) to end (8 sts).

Break off yarn and thread through remaining sts. Pull tight and secure. Join row ends.

Stuff lightly.

FINISHING OFF

Fold toy tidy to leave an opening two thirds of the way up. Sew side seams.

Sew arms, legs and hat onto Humpty.

Embroider eyes using C and French knots, and mouth using B and chain stitch. Embroider belt buckle using E and shoe buckles using C.

Hickory Dickory Dock nappy holder

Soft chunky wool in double moss stitch is used for the base of the container, with baby merino DK for the clock face. This project is not just for practical storage as the clock can also be detached and played with.

YOU WILL NEED

Garnstudio Eskimo, 100% wool
(54yd/49m per 50g ball)
7 balls Off White (shade 01) (A)
Garnstudio Baby Merino DK, 100% wool
(191yd/175m per 50g ball)
1 ball each of:
Off White (shade 02) (B)
Light Grey (shade 22) (C)
Lime (shade 09) (D)
Light Turquoise (shade 10) (E)
Yellow (shade 04) (F)
Small amount of red and dark brown yarn
for embroidery
5.5mm (US9:UK5) and 6mm (US10:UK4)
circular needle

A pair each of 3.75mm (US5:UK9) and 6mm
(US10:UK4) needles
Two double-pointed 3.75mm (US5:UK9) needles
Toy stuffing
Small pieces of hook-and-loop fastener

FINISHED SIZE

12in (30cm) diameter, 8in (20cm) deep

TENSION

Container: 13 sts and 20 rows to 4in (10cm)
over pattern using 6mm needles.
Clock: 24 sts and 32 rows to 4in (10cm) over
st st using 3.75mm needles.

CONTAINER

With 6mm needles and A, cast on 5 sts.
Next row: Inc in each of next 2 sts, k1, inc in each of next 2 sts (9 sts).
Row 1 and every following alt row: P to end.
Row 2: (K1, m1) to last st, k1 (17 sts).
Row 4: (K2, m1) to last st, k1 (25 sts).
Row 6: (K3, m1) to last st, k1 (33 sts).
Continue in this way increasing 8 sts on 12 foll right-side rows (129 sts).
Row 31: Purl to end.
Change to 6mm circular needle and use yarn double.
Mark the end of this row with a coloured thread for the end of the base.
Cont in rounds to form sides.
Next round: K3, (k2tog, k4) to end (108 sts).
Next round: P to end to form edge of base.
Next round: K to end.
Next round: P to end.
Working in double moss st, continue as follows:
Rounds 1 and 2: (K1, p1) to end.
Rounds 3 and 4: (P1, k1) to end.
These 4 rounds form the double moss st and are repeated throughout.
Continue straight until work measures 6in (15cm) from marker.
Change to 5.5mm circular needle.
Next round: P to end.
Next round: K to end.
Next round: P to end.
Cast off knitwise.
With WS facing, gather around cast-on edge and pull up tightly.
Join base seam.

CLOCK
Front

With 3.75mm needles and B cast on 5 sts.
Next row: Inc in each of next 2 sts, k1, inc in each of next 2 sts (9 sts).

Row 1 and every following alt row: P to end.
Row 2: (K1, m1) to last st, k1 (17 sts).
Row 4: (K2, m1) to last st, k1 (25 sts).
Row 6: (K3, m1) to last st, k1 (33 sts).
Continue in this way, increasing 8 sts on 6 foll right-side rows (81 sts).
Row 20: P to end.
Break off B.
Join in E.
Continue in this way, increasing 8 sts on 4 foll right-side rows (113 sts).
Purl 2 rows.
Next row: (K14, m1) to last st, k1 (121 sts).

Back

Purl 2 rows.
Next row: (K13, skpo) to last st, k1 (113 sts).
Next row and every following alt row: P to end.
Next row: (K12, skpo) to last st, k1 (105 sts).
Continue in this way, decreasing 8 sts on 3 foll right-side rows (81 sts).
Break off E.
Join in B.
Purl 1 row.
Next row: (K8, skpo) to last st, k1 (73 sts).
Next row and every following alt row: P to end.
Continue in this way, decreasing 8 sts on 8 foll right-side rows (9 sts).
Purl 1 row.
Next row: (K2tog) twice, k1, (k2tog) twice (5 sts).

Finishing the clock

Break off yarn and thread through sts. Fasten off tightly and join row ends, stuffing lightly as you go. Run gathering thread round cast-on sts, pull up tightly and fasten off. Using red embroidery thread, embroider French knots around face of clock and one in D at centre of clock. Embroider hands using chain stitch and E. Embroider top of hands in red and satin stitch.

SMALL PENDULUM DISCS
(make 2)
With 3.75mm needles and F cast on 5 sts.
Next row: Inc in each of next 2 sts, k1, inc in each of next 2 sts (9 sts).
Row 1 and every following alt row: P to end.
Row 2: (K1, m1) to last st, k1 (17 sts).
Row 4: (K2, m1) to last st, k1 (25 sts).
Row 6: (K3, m1) to last st, k1 (33 sts).
Purl 3 rows.
Next row: (K2, skpo) to last st, k1 (25 sts).
Next and every following alt row: P to end.
Next row: (K1, skpo) to last st, k1 (17 sts).
Next row: (Skpo) to last st, k1 (9 sts).
Next row: (K2tog) twice, k1, (k2tog) twice (5 sts).

Finishing the small pendulums
Break off yarn and thread through sts. Fasten off tightly and join row ends, stuffing lightly as you go. Run gathering thread round cast-on sts, pull up tightly and fasten off.

MOUSE
(starting at back)
With 3.75mm needles and C, cast on 6 sts.
Purl 1 row.
Next row: Inc in every st (12 sts).
Work in st st for 3 rows.
Next row: (K1, m1) to last st, k1 (23 sts).
Work in st st for 5 rows.
Next row: (K3, k2tog) 4 times, k3 (19 sts).
Next and every following alt row: P to end.
Next row: (K2, k2tog) 4 times, k3 (15 sts).
Next row: (K1, k2tog) to end (10 sts).
Next row: (K2tog) to end (5 sts).
Next row: K2tog, k1, k2tog (3 sts).
Break off yarn and thread through sts. Join row ends. Make a twisted cord for tail.

Ears
(make 2)
With 3.75mm needles and C, cast on 6 sts.
Purl 1 row.
Next row: (K2tog) 3 times.
Break off yarn and thread through sts.
Fasten off.

Finishing the mouse
Sew cast-off edges of mouse body together from back to front, stuffing firmly as you go. Attach ears and a tail made from a twisted cord. Embroider eyes using French knots in a dark brown.

LARGE PENDULUM DISC HANDLES
(make 2)
Using 3.75mm needles and F, cast on 5 sts.
Next row: Inc in each of next 2 sts, k1, inc in each of next 2 sts (9 sts).
Row 1 and every following alt row: P to end.
Row 2: (K1, m1) to last st, k1 (17 sts).
Row 4: (K2, m1) to last st, k1 (25 sts).
Continue in this way, increasing 8 sts on 3 foll right-side rows (49 sts).
Purl 3 rows.
Next row: (K4, skpo) to last st, k1 (41) sts.
Next and every following alt row: P to end.
Next row: (K3, skpo) to last st, k1 (33) sts.
Continue in this way, decreasing 8 sts on 3 foll right-side rows (9 sts).
Purl 1 row.
Next row: (K2tog) twice, k1, (k2tog) twice (5 sts).

Finishing the large pendulum
Break off yarn and thread through sts. Fasten off tightly and join row ends, stuffing lightly as you go. Run gathering thread round cast-on sts, pull up tightly and fasten off.

CORDS

(make one each of the following lengths: 7in/18cm, 6in/15cm and 5in/12cm)

Using 3.75mm double-pointed needles and D, cast on 4 sts.

Row 1: K to end, do not turn work.

Row 2: Slip sts to the other end of the needle, take yarn across back of work, pull tightly, k4, do not turn work.

Rep row 2 until cord is required length.

Next row: (K2tog) twice.

Next row: K2tog.

Fasten off.

FINISHING OFF

Sew large disc handles onto top of container, opposite each other and with half of the disc showing above top. Sew mouse and two smaller discs to end of cords. Sew pieces of hook-and-loop fastener to back of clock and container so that the clock can be removed.

Alternatives

Why not use the storage container without the clock in other rooms in the home? The clock will also make a fun toy on its own.

Three little pigs mobile

Pure wool is used for this fun mobile designed to hang in the nursery.
The chunky little piggies can fit inside the hut after playing when
it is time for both baby and piglets to go to sleep.

YOU WILL NEED
Debbie Bliss Rialto DK, 100% wool
(115yd/105m per 50g ball)
2 balls shade 29 (A)
1 ball each of shade 05 (B) and shade 26 (C)
A pair each of 2.75mm (US2:UK12) and 4mm
(US6:UK8) needles
A pair of size 2.75mm (US2:UK12)
double-pointed needles
Toy stuffing
4.5mm (USG/6:UK7) crochet hook

FINISHED SIZES
Hut: (not including roof) 4in (10cm) wide, 4$\frac{1}{2}$in
(11.5cm) high
Pigs: 3in (7.5cm) long

TENSION
20 sts and 40 rows to 4in (10cm) over garter st
using 4mm needles and yarn used double.

HUT
Walls

Made in one piece in garter st stripe.

Using 4mm needles and A doubled, cast on 26 sts.

Knit 3 rows.

Join in B.

Cont in garter st and stripes of 2 rows B and 4 rows A.

Repeat last 6 rows until 37 rows have been worked.

Place a marker at each end of row.

Work a further 11 rows in stripe patt.

Next row: (WS) Cast off 15 sts, k to end (11 sts).

Pattern a further 15 rows.

Next row: Cast on 15 sts, k to end (26 sts).

Continue working stripe pattern for a further 11 rows, place a marker at each end of row.

Work a further 37 rows.

Cast off knitwise.

Roof
(make in 3 pieces)

Using 4mm needles and A doubled, cast on 21 sts.

Cont in garter st and stripes of 5 rows A, (2 rows B and 4 rows A) to end.

Row 1: K to end.

Row 2: Skpo, k to last 2 sts, k2tog.

Row 3: K to end.

Rep rows 2 and 3 until 5 sts remain.

Alternatives

You could change the pigs for other animals or people for a fun variation. The hut and pigs can also be used separately as toys.

Next row: Skpo, k1, k2tog.

Next row: K to end.

Next row: Sl1, k2tog, psso.

Fasten off.

Base

Using 4mm needles and A doubled, cast on 21 sts.

Cont in garter st and stripes of 5 rows A, (2 rows B and 4 rows A) to end.

Rows 1 to 3: K to end.

Row 4: Skpo, k to last 2 sts, k2tog.

Row 5: K to end.

Row 6: Skpo, k to last 2 sts, k2tog.

Rows 7 and 8: K to end.

Rep last 3 rows once more.

Row 12: Skpo, k to last 2 sts, k2tog.

Row 13: K to end.

Rows 14 to 25: Rep rows 6 to 8 four more times.

Row 26: Skpo, k1, k2tog.

Row 27: K to end.

Row 28: Sl1, k2tog, psso.

Fasten off.

Chimney

Using 4mm needles and B doubled, cast on 7 sts.

Knit 11 rows.

Cast off knitwise.

PIGS
(make 3)

Body

Using 2.75mm needles and C, cast on 12 sts.

Row 1: (RS) K to end.

Row 2 and every alternate row: P to end.

Row 3: K2, (m1, k1) 8 times, k2 (20 sts).

Row 5: K1, (m1, k2) 9 times, m1, k1 (30 sts).

Row 7: K2, (m1, k3) 9 times, m1, k1 (40 sts).

Rows 9, 11, 13, 15 and 17: K to end.

Row 19: K1, (skpo, k2) 9 times, skpo, k1 (30 sts).
Row 21: K to end.
Row 23: (Skpo, k1) to end (20 sts).
Row 25: K to end.
Row 27: (K2tog) to end (10 sts).
Row 29: K to end.
Rows 30, 31 and 32: P to end.
Cut yarn, leaving a small length. Using a tapestry needle, thread through the remaining sts, pull tight and secure.

Ears

Using 2.75mm needles and C, cast on 7 sts.
Row 1: (RS) K to end.
Row 2 and every alternate row: P to end.
Row 3: Skpo, k3, k2tog.
Row 5: Skpo, k1, k2tog.
Row 7: Sl1, k2tog, psso.

Legs

Using a pair of size 2.75mm double-pointed needles and C, cast on 6 sts.
Row 1: K to end, do not turn work.
Row 2: Slip sts to the other end of the needle, take yarn across back of work, pull tightly, k6, do not turn work. Rep row 2 seven times more. Leave a length of yarn, thread through sts, pull tightly and fasten off.

CORDS
For pigs

(make one each in the following lengths: 9in/23cm, 8in/17cm and 6½in/17cm long)
Using a pair of size 2.75mm double-pointed needles and A, cast on 3 sts.
Row 1: K to end, do not turn work.
Row 2: Slip sts to the other end of the needle, take yarn across back of work, pull tightly, k3, do not turn work. Rep row 2 until cord is required length. Leave a length of yarn, thread through sts, pull tight. Do not cut yarn.

For hut

Using a pair of size 2.75mm double-pointed needles and A, cast on 4 sts.
Row 1: K to end, do not turn work.
Row 2: Slip sts to the other end of the needle, take yarn across back of work, pull tightly, k4, do not turn work.
Leave a length of yarn, thread through sts, pull tight and secure. Do not cut yarn.

FINISHING OFF
Hut

For the hut walls, sew cast-on edge to the cast-off-edge. Sew the 3 sides of the roof together using a flat seam. Position roof onto the top of the walls – the markers indicate the three sides of the house. Sew in place. Position the base as before, lining up the markers. Sew the cord for the hut onto the top of the roof. With the other end of the i-cord, fold over to form loop. Sew into place. This can be used to put onto a ceiling hook. Sew together the cast-on and cast-off edges of chimney. Slide over the cord, and sew into place to centre of roof.

Pigs

Sew up three quarters of the seam, and stuff pig firmly, then sew the rest of the seam. Place one ear each side of head, slip st into place with WS of ear facing. Fold ear over to RS and sew down cast-off end, allowing ear to bulge slightly. Using a single thread of B, embroider spots on body of pig using satin stitch. Embroider two diagonal lines on ends of snout. Embroider a French knot for each eye. For legs, stuff each one. Position on body and sew in place. For the tail, using B double and crochet hook, make a chain length of 2in (5cm) long. Fasten off. Sew one end to the pig, twist the tail. Sew cords to pigs, and sew to three corners of hut.

Bathroom

MARINE LIFE AND **NAUTICAL STRIPES** INSPIRE THE **FUN** PROJECTS IN THIS ROOM. MADE WITH PRACTICAL **COTTON** YARNS IN **FRESH** COLOURS, THESE ACCESSORIES ARE **QUIRKY** AND **ORIGINAL**.

Marine

Marine life pocket storage

Fish-bowl containers

Shell wash bag

life

Marine life pocket storage

Stripes, fish and starfish create a seaside theme in jaunty nautical colours. Practical cotton Aran is used for this handy pocket storage in which to tidy away all your bathroom bits and pieces.

YOU WILL NEED
Rico Creative Cotton Aran, 100% cotton (93yd/85m per 50g ball)
3 balls Dark Blue (shade 38) (A)
2 balls Natural (shade 60) (B)
1 ball Pistachio (shade 41) (C)
A pair of 4.5mm (US7:UK7) needles
2 pieces dowelling 18in (45cm) long

FINISHED SIZE
18in (45cm) wide x 18in (45cm) high

TENSION
18 sts and 24 rows to 4in (10cm) over st st using 4.5mm needles.

PATTERN NOTES
When working from chart, right-side rows are knit rows and read from right to left. Wrong-side rows are purl rows and read from left to right. Use separate balls of yarn for each area of colour and twist yarn on wrong side to avoid a hole when changing colour.

BASE

Using 4.5mm needles and A, cast on 80 sts.
Row 1: K1, p1, k to last 2 sts, p1, k1.
Row 2: K1, p to last st, k1.
These 2 rows form the st st with 2 sts in moss st at each end.
Work a further 8 rows.
Cont in stripe sequence of (2 rows B, 4 rows A) 19 times, 2 rows B, then 10 rows A.
Cast off.

POCKETS

Using 4.5mm needles and A, cast on 22 sts.
Make 5 fish pockets and 4 star pockets, following charts on pages 150–1.
Follow chart to end, working 2 rows moss st at top. Cast off in C.

FINISHING OFF

Press pieces according to yarn band instructions. Place pockets on main piece, pin and sew in place. Turn top and bottom of main piece over to back to form a hem. Cut dowelling to fit top and bottom and insert.

Alternatives

You could also make this project in one colour for bedroom or kitchen storage.

MARINE LIFE STORAGE FISH CHART

(22 sts x 32 rows)

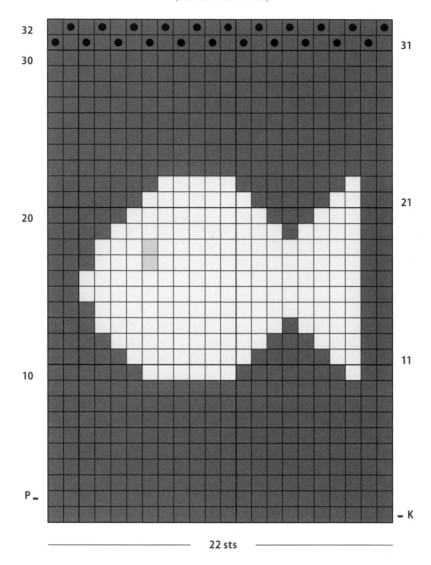

22 sts

Key to charts

	A Dark Blue		K on RS, P on WS
	B Natural	●	K on WS, P on RS
	C Pistachio		

1 square represents 1 stitch and 1 row

MARINE LIFE STORAGE STARFISH CHART

(22 sts x 32 rows)

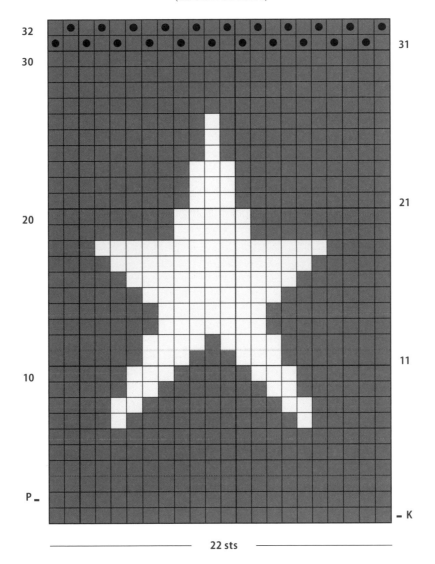

22 sts

Fish-bowl containers

Intarsia fish motifs swim in the waves on a neutral colour base to make these jolly bowl-shaped containers. Knitted in cotton Aran, these useful bathroom accessories are ideal for stashing anything from cotton-wool balls to face cloths.

YOU WILL NEED

Debbie Bliss Eco Aran Fairtrade Collection, 100% cotton (82yd/75m per 50g ball)
For both bowls
3 balls shade 605 (A)
1 ball each of shade 622 (B) and shade 601 (C)
Small bowl: A pair of 4.5mm (US7:UK7) needles
Large bowl: A pair of 5mm (US8:UK6) needles

PATTERN NOTES

Small bowl: Use 4.5mm needles and single yarn throughout.
Large bowl: Use 5mm needles and double yarn throughout.

FINISHED SIZES

Small: 6in (15cm) diameter, 4in (10cm) high
Large: 8in (20cm) diameter, 6in (15cm) high

TENSION

Small: 18 sts and 24 rows to 4in (10cm) over st st using 4.5mm needles.
Large: 16 sts and 22 rows to 4in (10cm) over st st using 5mm needles and yarn double.

Containers

Using 4.5mm needles (for small size), 5mm needles (for large size) and A, cast on 5 sts. Purl 1 row.

Next row: Inc in each of next 2 sts, k1, inc in each of next 2 sts (9 sts).

Next and every following wrong side row: P to end.

Row 1: K1, (m1, k1) to end (17 sts).
Row 3: K1, (m1, k2) to end (25 sts).
Row 5: K1, (m1, k3) to end (33 sts).
Row 7: K1, (m1, k4) to end (41 sts).
Row 9: K1, (m1, k5) to end (49 sts).
Row 11: K1, (m1, k6) to end (57 sts).
Row 13: K1, (m1, k7) to end (65 sts).
Row 14: K to end.

Sides

Row 15: K to end.
Row 16: P to end.
Row 17: K1, (m1, k8) to end (73 sts).
Row 18: P to end.
Row 19: K1, (m1, k9) to end (81 sts).

Next row: P to end, dec 1 st at centre of row (80 sts).

Work motif as follows in st st:
Row 1: K(8A, 4B) 6 times, 8A.
Row 2: P2B, (4A, 8B) 3 times, 4C (8B, 4A) 3 times, 2B.
Row 3: K(8B, 4A) twice, 7B, 1C, 4A, 1B, 7C, (4A, 8B) 3 times.
Row 4: P2A, (4B, 8A) twice, 4B, 4A, 10C, 3A, 2C, 1A, (4B, 8A) twice, 4B, 2A.
Row 5: K31A, 3C, 1A, 12C, 33A.
Row 6: P32A, 17C, 31A.
Row 7: K31A, 12C, 1A, 3C, 33A.
Row 8: P(8A, 4B) twice, 8A, 2B, 11C, 1B, 3C, 7A, (4B, 8A) twice.
Row 9: K2B, (4A, 8B) twice, 4A, 1B, 2C, 3B, 9C, 5B, (4A, 8B) twice, 4A, 2B.
Row 10: P(8B, 4A) 3 times, 1B, 6C, 1B, 4A, 1C, 7B, (4A, 8B) twice.
Row 11: K2A, (4B, 8A) 3 times, 4C, (8A, 4B) 3 times, 2A.
Row 12: With A only, p to end.

For large bowl only

Work 2 rows st st.

Both sizes

Shape top

Row 1: (K8, k2tog) to end (72 sts).
Rows 2 and 4: P to end.
Row 3: (K7, k2tog) to end (64 sts).
Row 5: (K6, k2tog) to end (56 sts).
Row 6: Knit.
Beg with a knit row, work 8 rows st st.
Cast off.

FINISHING OFF

Join seam.

Alternatives

Leave out the fish design and make in different colours for containers to suit any room or decor.

Shell
wash bag

Mercerized cotton is used for this pretty crochet wash bag.
Spiral shell motifs sit on the simple textured base, with a shell
handle adding to the seaside theme.

YOU WILL NEED

Rico Cotton Essentials DK, 100% cotton
(142yd/130m per 50g ball)
3 balls Natural (shade 51) (A)
1 ball each of:
Mint (shade 41) (B)
Pistachio (shade 86) (C)
2.5mm (USC/2:UK12) crochet hook

FINISHED SIZE

8$\frac{1}{2}$in (22cm) wide x 9$\frac{1}{2}$in (24cm) deep

TENSION

26 dc and 29 rows to 4in (10cm) over main
pattern using 2.5mm crochet hook.

FRONT AND BACK
(alike)
Using 2.5mm crochet hook and A, make 55 ch.
Foundation row: 1dc into 2nd ch from hook, 1dc into each dc to end, turn.
Row 1: 1ch, working into back loop only, work 1dc into each dc to end, turn (54 dc).
Rep last row until work measures 8in (20cm) ending with RS facing for next row, turn.
Eyelet row: 1ch, working into back loop only work 1dc into each of next 4dc, (2ch, miss next 2dc, 1dc into each of next 7dc) 5 times, 2ch, miss next 2dc, 1dc into each of last 3dc, turn.
Next row: 1dc into each dc and 2dc into each ch of the 2ch space, working all sts into the back loops as previously set by row 1 at beg of pattern. Cont until work measures 9$\frac{1}{2}$in (24cm) from foundation row, ending with a RS row.
Fasten off.

CORD
Using 2.5mm crochet hook and B, make a ch 28$\frac{1}{2}$in (72cm) long.
1dc into 2nd ch from hook, 1dc into each ch to end.
Fasten off.

HANDLE
Using 2.5mm crochet hook and B, make 110 ch.
Foundation row: Work 1dc into 2nd ch from hook, then 1dc into each ch to end, turn (109 dc).
Row 1: (RS) 1ch, 1dc into 1st dc, (miss 2 dc, 5tr into next dc, miss next 2dc, 1dc into next dc) 18 times. Fasten off.
Turn work so that the WS of last row is facing, and with base of dcs facing upwards.
Rejoin yarn to right-hand side, 1ch, 1dc into each ch to end, turn (109 dc).
Row 1: (RS) 1ch, 1dc into 1st dc, (miss 2dc, 5tr into next dc, miss next 2dc, 1dc into next dc) 18 times. Fasten off.

SHELLS
(make 3)
Using 2.5mm crochet hook and C, make a circle by wrapping yarn around finger, make a ch over the yarn to form a ring.
Work 8dc into ring, pull yarn tight to form a small ring.
Working in continuous rounds to form a spiral, work as follows:
Working into back loops only 2htr into each of next 5 sts, 2tr into each of next 9 sts, 2dtr into each of next 7 sts, 1dtr into next st, 2dtr into next st, 1dtr into next st, 4ch, sl st into base of previous dtr.
Fasten off.

FINISHING OFF
Press pieces according to yarn band instructions.
Sew up sides and bottom edge of wash bag.
Place shells across front and sew in place.
Sew on handle. Thread cord through eyelets to tie at side.

Alternatives

This bag can also be used as a travel or cosmetics bag. Alternatively, make without the shells for extra bedroom storage.

Basic techniques

THE FOLLOWING PAGES TAKE YOU THROUGH THE **BASICS**, INCLUDING **GETTING STARTED**, BASIC **KNITTING** AND **CROCHET** TECHNIQUES. PARTICULAR METHODS USED FOR SOME OF THE PROJECTS, SUCH AS **INTARSIA**, **FELTING** AND **EMBROIDERY** ARE ALL EXPLAINED HERE.

Getting started

ALTERNATIVES

For each project, there are suggestions for other ways to use the pattern to create alternative items. A more individual result can be achieved by changing colour combinations or yarns too.

YARN SUBSTITUTION

Choosing a yarn is part of the pleasure of knitting and crochet. Substituting a yarn will make the project more individual to you but there are a couple of points to remember. If you change yarns, make sure that the substitute one is the same weight as the original, and also knits to the same tension, as a different one will change the measurements of the item. Check the ball band for yardage too, as any difference may mean that you need more or fewer balls of yarn. Bear in mind the function of the item you are making too. For example, for projects for a baby, a really soft, smooth yarn is important. For rooms such as the bathroom, cotton works better than wool.

TENSION SWATCHES

Making a tension swatch is a good idea before starting any project, to see if you need to change needle sizes to achieve the correct tension. If you are substituting yarn, it will also help to give you an idea of how the finished project will look.

READING PATTERNS

Before starting to knit, read through the pattern carefully. Check through the abbreviations that the pattern uses, especially ones that you are less familiar with.

FOLLOWING CHARTS

There are quite a few colourwork charts in the book. As with all knitting charts, one square represents one stitch, and a row of squares a row of knitting. On a RS row follow the chart from right to left, and on a WS row begin from left to right. Knitting starts in the bottom right-hand corner. Refer to the colour key for which colours to use. Using a chart ruler is a good idea or, alternatively, photocopy the chart and mark off each row knitted.

Knitting techniques

CASTING ON

1 Make a loop on the left-hand needle, and secure with a slip knot. Holding the needle with the loop in your left hand, take the right-hand needle and insert it through the loop from front to back. Wrap the yarn around the right-hand needle.

2 Draw the yarn under and through to create a new loop. Slip this onto the left-hand needle.

3 Repeat until you have the correct number of stitches for the pattern.

CASTING OFF

1 Work the first two stitches of the cast-off row, pass the first stitch over the top of the second stitch and off the needle.

2 Repeat until one stitch remains. Cut yarn and thread through the last stitch and pull to secure.

1

2

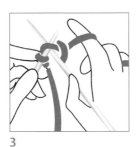

3

1

2

KNIT STITCH (K)

1 After cast-on row, hold needle with cast-on stitches in left hand. Insert right-hand needle into first stitch and wrap yarn around, yarn held at back of work.

2 Pull the yarn through, creating a new loop.

3 Slip new stitch onto right-hand needle. Continue to end of row.

PURL STITCH (P)

1 Hold the yarn at the front of the work.

2 Place the right-hand needle into the first stitch from front to back. Wrap the yarn around right-hand needle anti-clockwise.

3 Bring the needle back through the stitch and pull through.

1

1

2

2

3

3

OTHER STITCHES

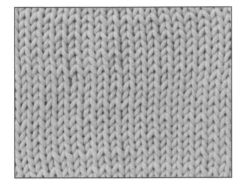

Stocking stitch
K on RS rows, P on WS rows.

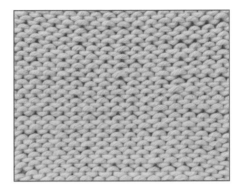

Reverse stocking stitch
K on WS rows, P on RS rows.

Moss stitch
Worked on an even number
of stitches.
Row 1: (K1, p1) to end.
Row 2: (P1, k1) to end.
Repeat these two rows.

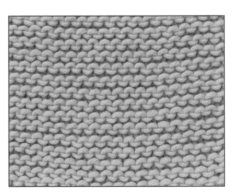

Garter stitch
K on every row.

CABLES

Using a cable needle, cables are formed over varied numbers of stitches by crossing one set of stitches over another.

Basic 4-stitch cable (C4F)

Worked on reverse stocking stitch.

1 Slip next 2 sts onto a cable needle and hold at front of work.

2 Knit the next 2 sts from the left-hand needle, then K2 sts from the cable needle.

The same cable can be worked as C4B, holding the stitches on the cable needle at the back of work instead of the front.

1
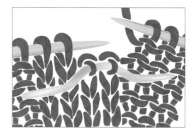

2
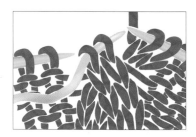

INTARSIA

This method is used for larger areas of colourwork than Fair Isle, where the yarn is not taken across the back of the work. Separate balls of yarn are used, or smaller amounts wound onto bobbins. When a new colour is introduced into a row, twist the two yarns together at the back of work. After knitting, press according to the yarn band instructions to neaten the join.

FELTING

After knitting and sewing up, put the item to be felted into a pillowcase and sew up the top. Put into a washing machine set at 140°F (60°C). Wash, but do not tumble dry. Pull into shape, putting objects into containers to help with shaping, and leave to dry.

Crochet techniques

CHAIN STITCH (CH)

1 After making a slip knot, wrap the yarn over the hook from back to front. Pull the yarn taut.

2 Draw the yarn through to form a new loop.

3 Make as many base chains as the pattern requires.

1   2   3

SLIP STITCH (SL ST)

Insert the hook into the second chain from hook. Wrap the yarn over the hook, and draw yarn through the work and the loop in one movement. One slip stitch completed. Repeat as required.

DOUBLE CROCHET (DC)

1 Insert hook into work (2nd chain from hook), wrap yarn over hook and draw through the work.

2 Wrap yarn again and draw yarn through both loops on the hook. 1 dc completed. Repeat as required.

1

2

HALF TREBLE (HTR)

1 Wrap yarn around hook and insert into work (3rd ch from hook).

2 Wrap yarn over hook, draw through the work only, and wrap yarn again. Draw through all 3 loops on hook.

1

2

TREBLE (TR)

1 Wrap yarn around hook and then place into a stitch.

2 Wrap yarn around hook and then draw the loop through (three loops should now be on the hook).

3 Catch the yarn and draw through two of the loops.

4 Catch yarn again and draw it through the remaining two loops.

1

2

3

4

Finishing touches

FRENCH KNOTS

1 Bring the needle from the back to the front of work to the point you want to place the knot. Twist yarn around needle a few times, depending on the size of knot required.

2 Insert needle back into the work, keeping yarn wrapped around needle tightly. Feed the yarn through the twists just made. Secure at back of work.

CHAIN STITCH

Make a knot to secure yarn at back of work. Bring the needle to the front. Insert needle near the starting point, and bring it out again a short distance away, leaving it in the fabric. Wrap yarn underneath needle. Pull needle out to form a chain. Repeat as required.

SATIN STITCH

Make a knot to secure yarn at back of work. Bring needle to front of work. Insert needle from front to back, forming a stitch the length required. Repeat until there are enough stitches for the motif you are doing.

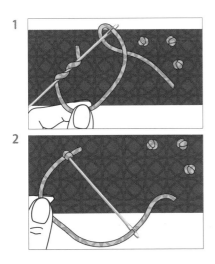

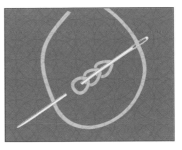

chain stitch

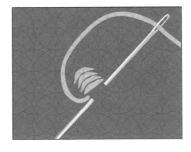

satin stitch

Sewing up

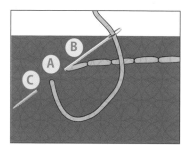

MATTRESS STITCH

Use mattress stitch for an invisible seam and
a neat finish. After pressing, place the pieces
side by side with RS facing. Starting at the
bottom, secure the yarn and bring the needle
up between the first and second stitch on one
piece. Find the corresponding point on the
other piece, and insert the needle there. Keep
the sewing-up yarn loose as you work up the
seam, then pull tight.

BACKSTITCH

Make a knot to secure yarn at back of work.
Bring the needle up at point A, insert at point B,
and bring back up at point C. Repeat, keeping
the stitches at an even length.

ABBREVIATIONS

C4[6]B	cable 4[6] back: slip next 2[3] sts onto a cable needle and hold at back of work, k2[3], then k2[3] from cable needle
C4[6]F	cable 4[6] front: slip next 2[3] sts onto a cable needle and hold at front of work, k2[3], then k2[3] from cable needle
ch	chain stitch
CN1	make 1 cob nut: k1 without slipping st off left needle, yf, then k1 again into same st
cont	continue
Cr2L	cross 2 left: slip next st onto a cable needle and leave at front of work, k1, then k1 from cable needle
Cr2Lp	cross 2 left purlwise: slip next st onto a cable needle and leave at front of work, p1, then k1 from cable needle.
Cr2R	cross 2 right: slip next st on cable needle and leave at back of work, k1, then k1 from cable needle
Cr2Rp	cross 2 right purlwise: slip next st on a cable needle and leave at back of work, k1, then p1 from cable needle.
Cr3L	cross 3 left: slip next 2 sts onto cable needle and hold at front of work, p1, then k2 from cable needle
Cr3R	cross 3 right: slip next st onto cable needle and hold at back of work, k2, then p1 from cable needle
Cr4L	cross 4 left: slip next 3 sts onto cable needle and hold at front of work, p1, then k3 from cable needle
Cr4R	cross 4 right: slip next st onto cable needle and hold at back of work, k3, then p1 from cable needle
Cr5L	cross 5 left: slip next 3 sts onto cable needle and hold at front of work, p2, then k3 from cable needle
Cr5R	cross 5 right: slip next 2 sts onto cable needle and hold at back of work, k3, then p2 from cable needle
dc	double crochet
dc2tog	leaving last loop of each st on hook, work 1dc in each of next 2 sts, yrh, draw through all 3 loops on hook

dec	decrease
dtr	double treble
g st	garter stitch, every row knit
htr	half treble
inc	increase by working twice into stitch
k	knit
k2tog	knit two stitches together
m1	make 1 st by picking up the bar between the st just worked and the next st on left-hand needle then k into the back of it
MB	make bobble: k into front, back, front and back of next st, (turn, p4, turn, k4) twice, then pass 2nd, 3rd and 4th sts over the first to complete the bobble.
Mb	make bobble, (k2, turn, p2, turn) twice, (k next st tog with corresponding st on 1st row of bobble) twice to complete.
MK	make knot: (k1, p1, k1, p1, k1, p1) all in next st, pass 2nd, 3rd, 4th, 5th and 6th sts over the first to complete the knot
p	purl
p2tog	purl 2 sts together
p3tog	purl 3 sts together
psso	pass slipped st over
rev st st	reverse stocking stitch, p on right side and k on wrong side
RS	right side of work
skpo	sl1, k1, then pass slipped stitch over
sl	slip
ss	slip stitch
st(s)	stitch(es)
st st	stocking stitch, k on RS and p on WS
tbl	through the back of the loop
tr	treble
TW2l	twist 2 left: k into back of 2nd st on left needle, then into front of first st and slip both sts off the needle together
WS	wrong side of work
yf	yarn forward
yrh	yarn round hook
yrn	yarn round needle to make a stitch
( )	repeat instructions inside brackets

SUPPLIERS LIST

Alpaca Select
www.alpaca-select.com
email: sales@alpaca-select.com
tel: +44 (0)2476 411776

Artesano Ltd
www.artesanoyarns.co.uk
email : info@artesanoyarns.co.uk
tel: +44 (0)1189 503350

Designer Yarns Ltd
www.designeryarns.uk.com
email: enquiries@designeryarns.uk.com
tel: +44 (0)1535 664222

Garnstudio
www.garnstudio.com
email: export@garnstudio.com
tel: +47 23 30 32 20

Scandinavian Knitting Design Yarns Ltd
www.scandinavianknittingdesign.com
email: sales@scandinavianknittingdesign.com
tel: +44 (0)1189 884226

Rico
www.rico-design.co.uk

Sirdar Spinning Ltd (also for Sublime)
www.sirdar.co.uk
email: consumer@sirdar.co.uk
tel: 01924 231682.

Texere Yarns Ltd
www.texere-yarns.co.uk
email: info@texere.co.uk
tel: +44 (0)1274 722191

CONVERSIONS

NEEDLE SIZES

UK	Metric	US
14	2mm	0
13	2.5mm	1
12	2.75mm	2
11	3mm	–
10	3.25mm	3
–	3.5mm	4
9	3.75mm	5
8	4mm	6
7	4.5mm	7
6	5mm	8
5	5.5mm	9
4	6mm	10
3	6.5mm	10.5
2	7mm	10.5
1	7.5mm	11
0	8mm	11
00	9mm	13
000	10mm	15

CROCHET HOOKS

UK	Metric	US
14	2mm	B/1
13	2.25mm	–
12	2.5mm	C/2
11	3mm	–
10	3.25mm	D/3
9	3.5mm	E/4
8	4mm	G/6
7	4.5mm	–
6	5mm	H/8
5	5.5mm	I/9
4	6mm	J/10
3	6.5mm	K/10.5
2	7mm	–
0	8mm	L/11
00	9mm	M–N/13
000	10mm	N–P/15

UK/US YARN WEIGHTS

UK	US
2-ply	Lace
3-ply	Fingering
4-ply	Sport
Double knitting (DK)	Light worsted
Aran	Fisherman/worsted
Chunky	Bulky
Super chunky	Extra bulky

UK/US CROCHET TERMS

UK	US
Slip stitch	Slip stitch
Double crochet	Single crochet
Half treble	Half double crochet
Treble	Double crochet
Double treble	Triple crochet
Treble treble	Double triple crochet

Project index

LOUNGE

Knotted rope
cable throw

Felted storage
containers

Pebbles draught
excluder

DINING ROOM

Berries felted
fruit bowl

Textured place
mats & coasters

Poinsettia napkin
holders

KITCHEN

Pansies shopper

English rose
tea cozy

Basket-stitch
mug cozies

GARDEN

Ploughed fields
patchwork throw

Grain & ridge
plant pot holders

Large leaf
cushion cover

MAIN BEDROOM

Circle patches bedcover

Rosette cushion cover

Textured hot water
bottle cover

GUEST BEDROOM

Flower squares
bedcover

Diamond bolster
cushion

Flower & check
lavender bags

SECRET GARDEN BEDROOM

Butterfly & flower
curtain

Butterfly cushion
cover

Hearts & flowers
toy bag

PIRATE'S BEDROOM

Seaweed door
curtain

Anchor floor
cushion

Jolly Roger
toy bag

NURSERY

Humpty Dumpty
toy tidy

Hickory Dickory Dock
nappy holder

Three little
pigs mobile

BATHROOM

Marine life pocket storage

Fish-bowl containers

Shell wash bag

ABOUT THE AUTHOR

Sian Brown fell in love with yarn and knitting while studying for her BA in Fashion and Textiles in Cheltenham, UK. She went on to become a knitwear designer, freelancing for commercial companies that supply the high street stores and for swatch companies selling design ideas to the US. Sian has taught at the London College of Fashion on their knitwear course. She now lives in Hastings, on the south coast of England, and designs handknits for several magazines and yarn companies. She is a regular contributor to *Knitting* magazine. www.sianbrown.com

PUBLISHER'S ACKNOWLEDGEMENTS

GMC Publications would like to thank Diana Mothersole, Jo Pallett and Rosie Darlison for lending us props; the owners and pets of the beautiful homes where we photographed the projects and Tim Clinch for the stunning photography and all his additional help.

AUTHOR'S ACKNOWLEDGEMENTS

Thanks to the following at GMC: to Gerrie Purcell for commissioning the book, and giving me a great deal of creative freedom. To Virginia Brehaut for her editorial skills, and to Gilda Pacitti and Rebecca Mothersole for styling and art direction. Thanks also to Tim Clinch for the stunning photography.

To my pattern writer Penny Hill for her technical skills and many years of a great working relationship. To my team of knitters, with special thanks to Janet Morton and Jenny Shore, for their patience and creative knitting skills, and fearless reaction to phone calls starting with...I know you're really busy but... and ending with...and the deadline is....

To the companies that kindly donated yarn and their patience and helpfulness throughout the process: Alpaca Select, Artesano, Designer Yarns, Rico, Sirdar, Scandinavian Knitting Design Yarns and Texere.

Lastly, a personal thanks to my daughters Hannah and Rhiannon, who have grown up with a working mum surrounded by endless piles of yarn, listened to many years of discussions about designs, helped by adding to the sketches as toddlers, and by giving advice later. All this while never looking as if they have lost the will to live. I hope that I have not put them off either knitting or motherhood.

INDEX
Project names are shown in italics

To place an order, or to request a catalogue, contact:

GMC Publications, Castle Place, 166 High Street,
Lewes, East Sussex, BN7 1XU, United Kingdom
Tel: +44 (0)1273 488005 Fax: +44 (0)1273 402866
www.gmcbooks.com